CLASSROOM MANAGEMENT: Principles to Practice

How to manage a class is probably the major worry of all teachers in training and young teachers new to the profession. Worries about behaviour management are important but so too are worries about the choice and presentation of material. Educational psychology offers much which can help young teachers but all too often books about educational psychology concentrate on theory without showing how good classroom practice should emerge from this. This book, however, shows how psychological principles, strategies and techniques can be applied to improve classroom practice. This book uses practical examples as illustrations; it does not merely offer a series of 'recipes' for the teacher but provides a comprehensive framework for positive classroom management.

Shirley L. Bull is an Educational Psychologist in the West Midlands.

Jonathan E. Solity is a Lecturer in Psychology and Children with Special Needs, University of Warwick.

The authors both have extensive primary teaching experience.

Classroom Management:

PRINCIPLES TO PRACTICE

SHIRLEY BULL AND JONATHAN SOLITY

R

ROUTLEDGE
London & New York

First published 1987 by Croom Helm
Reprinted 1989 by Routledge
11 New Fetter Lane, London EC4P 4EE
29 West 35th Street, New York, NY 10001

© 1987 Shirley Bull and Jonathan Solity

Printed and bound in Great Britain by Mackays of Chatham PLC

British Library Cataloguing in Publication Data

Bull, Shirley
    Classroom management: principles to practice.
    1. Classroom management
    I. Title II. Solity, Jonathan
    371.1′024   LB3013

    ISBN 0 415 04286 0

Library of Congress Cataloging in Publication Data

Bull, Shirley,
    Classroom management.

    Includes index.
    1. Classroom management. 2. Teaching. 3. Teacher-
student relationships. I. Solity, Jonathan. II. Title.
LB3013.B85   1987   371.1′02   87-8942

ISBN 0 415 04286 0

Contents

Acknowledgements

There are several groups of people we should like to thank for their time, help and advice during the preparation of this book: Alan Hedge and Mick Pitchford for sharing ideas and information with us; Harry Bull, Joan Figg and Audrey Pugh for their comments on draft copies of the manuscript. In particular we would express our thanks to Ted Raybould for his encouragement and advice, his attention to detail and stimulating discussion about various conceptual issues. However, responsibility for the views expressed and for any errors and omissions remains, of course, entirely our own.

We are indebted to Ann Hope, Lyn Beddowes, Linda Osbourn and Margaret Key for their patience and for their fluent and accurate typing at different stages in the preparation. Our thanks to Nick Fenwick for helping to proof read the manuscript. Finally and most important of all, we wish to thank Harry, Marian, our families and friends for their encouragement, support and patience while this book was being written.

Shirley L. Bull
Jonathan E. Solity

Authors' Note

In examples which are based on real situations, names have been altered to protect the anonymity of those concerned. Throughout this book male and female titles and names, and the words she and he, are used randomly. In referring to both teachers and children 'she' and 'he' may be used interchangeably.

Psychology provides teachers with some factual information to think about, some conceptual models to think with and some techniques for getting further information about their children.

Chris Reeve

Preface

Classroom Management: Principles to Practice provides practical guidance on how to make classroom management effective and enjoyable.

Rather than presenting 'tips' for teachers, we offer a framework for thinking about and planning day-to-day practice in class. We describe an overall approach to classroom management which can be used in a wide range of teaching settings. Yet the approach can be tailored to the specific requirements of each.

Does a business-like yet positive classroom atmosphere just 'happen'? How can a teacher promote good behaviour from the outset with a new class? What can be done to minimise the risk that children will misbehave? What does a teacher do to keep children working hard and behaving well? How can misbehaviours be handled constructively? These are some of the questions we address.

Our central theme is the development of a *positive system of management*. We focus on factors which are within a teacher's sphere of influence, and concentrate on how teachers can organise the classroom environment to encourage pupils' appropriate behaviour and progress. The book is teacher-centred rather than child-centred — we emphasise what the *teacher* does, and draw out the implications for pupils.

In Part One we start with first principles. Chapter 1 introduces the model of learning and behaviour on which the book is based: the behavioural model. Within education, the behavioural model is often associated with approaches designed to overcome pupils' learning difficulties or behaviour problems. However, this book represents a major departure from that theme. Instead we describe how a behavioural approach can be used *in general classroom practice: with all the children in a class.* For the model offers teachers an *overall* perspective on teaching and management which is clear, practical and, perhaps most important of all, is positive in its philosophy. In Chapter 2 we use the model to develop a framework for classroom management which will encourage children to behave in constructive ways. Chapter 3 outlines a behavioural framework for teaching and its implications for the teaching role.

In Parts Two and Three we show how principles outlined in Part One can be put into practice.

Part Two deals with getting 'good' behaviour started. We examine the classroom from three different directions. First we describe how the classroom itself can be organised so that it helps, rather than hinders, the teacher and encourages children to work well on activities of different kinds (Chapter 4). We then offer some practical advice about managing the social context for children's behaviour (Chapter 5). In particular we discuss a teacher's role as leader, and ways teachers can affect children's behaviour through their *own* behaviour in this role. Chapter 6 explores the important part which a teacher's presentation and arrangement of learning activities plays in encouraging appropriate behaviour. Teaching time should be both effective and enjoyable.

Part Three is concerned with consequences of various kinds. Chapters 7 and 8 describe the consequences a teacher can provide so as to teach appropriate behaviours effectively and maintain them, once established. Then, since we cannot hope that unwanted behaviours will be eliminated altogether, these are considered in Chapter 9. We offer guidelines as to how to deal with misbehaviours and preserve a positive teacher–pupil relationship. One of the strengths of a behavioural approach is that it helps teachers to be more objective and accurate in their assessment of classroom events. Chapter 10 outlines ways of checking that any changes to management do really lead to improvements for the children concerned and the class as a whole. Steps a teacher can take to assess the seriousness of a child's difficult behaviour are also considered, for factual information can help put the problem in perspective and assist decisions about what is to be done.

A system of management would fall far short of requirements if it did not further teachers' long-term goals for children. We therefore conclude by discussing how a teacher using a positive system of management can be seen as helping children to derive personal satisfaction from learning and relationships in school (Chapter 11). We show how, in time, children can be taught to manage their own behaviour, rather than relying on their teacher to do it for them!

Throughout the book there are practical examples which illustrate how the principles of effective management can be applied to every-day situations. Whilst most of these are drawn from the primary school setting, the principles and basic practice we describe can be applied across different age ranges and educational settings.

Classroom Management: Principles to Practice is written for teachers in initial training and for qualified teachers who seek to enhance their existing good practice. The book will also be of interest to members of related professions who wish to become more familiar with the principles of behavioural psychology as applied to classroom practice.

Part One

First Principles

1

The Behavioural Model

INTRODUCTION

To begin thinking about and planning classroom practice we need a framework: an overall perspective which gives us both a start point and a sense of direction. The behavioural model offers a particular perspective on the teaching process which is clear and practical and perhaps most important of all, is positive in its philosophy. It provides teachers with a systematic way of describing and interpreting the classroom environment. It directs attention to key questions within the field of education, relating to how children learn and how teachers can maximise their effectiveness in the classroom.

This approach is concerned with the question, 'How do we learn to behave in the ways we do?' More specifically, when in the classroom (because this is the area with which we are concerned in this book) how do teachers and children learn to behave in the ways they do? These questions can be taken a step further when we ask how teachers and children influence each other's behaviour in the educational and social settings they share.

There are several key concepts and assumptions associated with the behavioural model (Table 1.1) which encapsulate a powerful and optimistic framework within which to work as teachers. They set the scene for teachers and children to experience and share a positive and successful working environment.

Table 1.1: Key concepts and assumptions associated with the behavioural approach

---

(1) Behaviour is learned
(2) Focus on the observable
(3) Learning means changing behaviour
(4) There is no teaching without learning
(5) Our behaviour is governed by the setting in which it occurs (setting events)
(6) Our behaviour is also governed by what follows our actions (consequences)

KEY CONCEPTS IN THE BEHAVIOURAL APPROACH

Behaviour is learned

The behavioural model centres on the relationship between behaviour and environment. Its principal tenet is that behaviour is learned and that what we learn and the ways in which we behave depend upon our everyday experience and the environment in which we live.

In the course of a single day, children encounter different environments. They spend time in school, in their own homes and those of friends, out at clubs of various sorts, the football ground and so on. The children learn certain behaviours from each of these environments and, as a teacher, you cannot affect what they learn from all of them. However, in so far as *you* determine what happens within your classroom, you can and do influence the environmental factors from which children learn. Indeed your classroom environment is, in a sense, an artificial one which is especially designed to teach children a wide range of educational skills and information. Your major role as teacher is to organise it in such a way as to result in successful learning experiences for your pupils.

Focus on the observable

We are all well practised at interpreting the actions of others, treating the way they behave as an outward indication of what they think and how they feel, as expressions of their attitudes and values, and so on. When we say that someone is 'upset', 'excited' or 'irritable', we are making suppositions about how they feel from our observations of their behaviour. Similarly, a teacher may say that a pupil 'lacks confidence', is 'lazy' or 'enjoys reading'. Again these comments express the teacher's interpretations of her pupil's behaviour, rather than describing what the child actually does.

Since our interpretations of other peoples' behaviour are essentially personal, they are likely to be coloured by our own expectations and values. Thus, two teachers may react differently to the same behaviour by a pupil, depending on the way they see it and on their expectations. One may read a child's smile on reprimand as 'insolent'; another may suppose that it is a 'nervous' smile or a sign of embarrassment. These different personal views may result in quite dissimilar ways of handling the same situation. Moreover, the influence which teacher expectations can have on pupil performance is well documented (Rosenthal and Jacobson, 1968; Pidgeon, 1970; Barker-Lunn, 1970; Elashoff and Snow, 1971; Hargreaves, 1972; Burns, 1982). So it is important for pupils that we try as far as possible to take a more objective view of their performance and behaviour in class.

Subjective interpretations of behaviour also tend to be vague and open to problems of miscommunication. Take, for example, the blanket terms 'disruptive' or 'aggressive' which a teacher may use to describe a child's behaviour in class. The assumption is that these words mean the same to everybody. However, a number of different behaviours could be covered by the blanket term 'disruptive'. Does the teacher mean the child was humming, talking out of turn, throwing paper darts, knocking over chairs or perhaps some other behaviour? He may mean that the child behaved in one way on Monday and in a different way on Tuesday. The picture of events held by the teacher may therefore look quite different from the point of view of the colleague or parent to whom he is talking.

The assumptions we make when using such blanket terms can equally lead to miscommunication between teacher and pupils about the way they should behave. If a teacher tells her pupils to 'Stop messing about' or 'Settle down', she assumes that her pupils share her understanding as to what exactly she means. But do they? These expressions are ambiguous and at least some of her pupils may fail to comply simply because they are uncertain about what their teacher wants them to do.

Miscommunication can also occur when describing children's learning in terms of what they 'understand' or 'know'. For example, a teacher might say, 'Michael *knows* numbers to six'. Does this mean that Michael can *count by rote* to six, or *match* numerals 1 to

5

6 to their equivalent sets of objects? Can he *point* to numerals 1 to 6 when the teacher names each of them, or perhaps *write* numerals 1 to 6 on dictation? Any one of these behaviours, all of them, or indeed others, may be what the teacher means. Moreover, unless she is clear about what Michael can do, she may inadvertently mislead herself when planning the next stage of his learning, the colleague who receives him and his record card next year, or his parents when they enquire about their child's progress on Open Night.

The behavioural approach and its concern with the observable can help us to make sure that our own reactions to events and our communication of these to others are as accurate as possible. The model directs us to deal only with those events and actions which can be seen and heard and are measurable. We therefore focus on what the children *do*, rather than how we interpret their behaviour. Examples of non-behavioural descriptions and some possible behavioural alternatives are shown in Table 1.2.

Table 1.2: Some non-behavioural and behavioural descriptions

Non-behavioural	Behavioural
A polite child	Says, 'Please' and 'Thank you' at appropriate times. Smiles and says 'Hello Miss' when first entering class. Raises hand to ask or tell. Asks permission to leave seat; or borrow a rubber . . . etc.
Concentrates well during story	Looks at teacher throughout a ten minute story. Afterwards, correctly answers questions about the story. After story, writes story in own words.
Has retention problems	Read all ten flashcards correctly three times on Friday. On Monday, read only five correctly on three occasions.
He's very aggressive today	Hit three children during morning break. Swore at John when he knocked his chair. Pushed to the front of the queue every time we lined up.

Confining yourself to the observable may initially seem unfamiliar and it certainly requires practice in order to minimise the effects of subjective interpretations and judgements on the way you deal with children's behaviour. However, the advantages of taking this view are many. You will avoid the trap of labelling children. You will see events within the classroom environment more clearly and will increase the clarity of your communication to your pupils, their parents and your colleagues.

Learning means changing behaviour

Within the behavioural model learning is indicated by a change in children's 'observable' behaviour. Thus the way we know that children have learned something is because we can see that their behaviour has altered. They may be able to follow a new routine, read new words or complete a new numerical operation. In each instance they can therefore be seen as having learned as a result of acquiring a new behaviour.

Changes in behaviour also occur when we no longer perform an activity which we had previously displayed. We might forget how to do something or we could replace a particular response with one we regard as more suitable and desirable. This happens frequently, for instance in the case of people who give up smoking. They change their behaviour by stopping smoking and so no longer engage in a potentially harmful activity.

There is no teaching without learning

The relationship between teaching and learning within the behavioural framework has been brought into sharp focus by Vargas (1977) when she wrote, 'Teaching is changing behaviour; it is helping others to learn faster or more efficiently than they would on their own' (p.6). The conclusion to be drawn from this statement is that teaching can only be said to have taken place when learning occurs. Teachers therefore directly facilitate this change of behaviour; they make learning possible through their interaction with pupils and ensure that children learn quicker than they would if left on their own.

However, it is equally important to note that learning can, and frequently does, occur in the absence of direct teaching. Pupils learn from a variety of sources both in and out of school, from peers and the events they see going on around them which do not involve the teacher. On many occasions nobody sets out with the clear intention of teaching but the children nevertheless learn. Much of what they learn is a result of their own curiosity and the routes of discovery on which they embark to explore and investigate their own world. So whereas we support the view that *there is no teaching without learning*, there is learning without teaching.

How the environment influences behaviour

According to the behavioural view, the environment operates in two principal ways to govern behaviour. First, it provides the circumstances in which behaviours take place: we never behave in a vacuum but always in the context of particular surroundings and in response to certain events. (Within the framework of the model we confine ourselves to identifiable, *external* events.) Here we shall refer to these contextual surroundings and events collectively as *setting events* (also referred to as *antecedents* in the literature) for behaviour. Secondly, the environment, including the people within it, provides the consequences which follow behaviour. Instances of a particular behaviour usually have some effect or outcomes and these *consequences* of our behaviour are important in determining how we will behave in future.

Thus we can look at behaviour within the context in which it occurs and the consequences which follow it:

Setting → Behaviour → Consequences
events
(antecedents)

If we imagine a slow-motion action-replay of single instances they might look something like the sequence of events illustrated in Table 1.3.

These events having happened, the consequences can act as the setting events for other behaviours. For example, once the room is light you may walk into it, the teacher's question to Mary is the cue for her to speak, etc. Thus, our behaviours and the external events surrounding them link together in a continuous chain of interactions. Let us now examine the sequence of 'setting events' — behaviour — consequences' more closely to see how the environmental events

Table 1.3: Some examples of interactions between environment and behaviour

	Setting events	Behaviour	Consequences
1.	The room is dark	Flick the light switch to 'on'	The room becomes light
2.	Teacher asks Paul a question	He says the correct answer	Teacher confirms as correct and praises Paul
3.	Lesson after break has started, teacher is talking to class	Mary walks into class	Teacher turns and frowns at Mary and asks why she is late
4.	An interschool cricket match, ball bowled to David	David hits ball clear to the boundary	His school supporters cheer; he scores 6 for his team: the captain praises him

Note: Example 1 shows how the behaviour may cause change simply in the physical environment. In example 2 the consequences are pleasant, but in example 3 they are less so. Example 4 illustrates the point that a single piece of behaviour may have several outcomes.

between which behaviours are sandwiched influence the ways in which we learn to behave.

The setting events

The setting events (antecedents) influence behaviour by containing cues which predispose us to behave in particular ways. They are important in governing where and when a behaviour occurs. To take an obvious example: on a sunny day you would be unlikely to walk about school wearing only a swimming costume, but on the beach it is different! Similarly, children are more likely to run and shout in a playground than in a classroom. We have noted that the term 'setting events' is used here to describe both the surroundings and the events which combine to set the scene for a particular behaviour.

Altering only one feature of these setting events can change the behaviour which occurs. Consider the situation in which an unfortunate young girl falls off her bicycle and grazes her knee. How she reacts to this event may differ according to whom she is with — regardless of *where* she is. If alone, she may get to her feet, pick up her bike and limp towards home. If with her schoolfriends, she may get up, manage to make a joke and even try to ride her bike away. However if she is surrounded by people who sympathise and console, she might be more likely to sit where she is and weep!

In the above example the cues provided by the setting events were obviously unplanned. However, when managing children's behaviour we can plan the cues provided by the environment so that the children are more likely to behave in ways which are desired or appropriate. For example, rather than suddenly realising that it is now bedtime and descending on the children to 'chivvy' them upstairs, a mother might first remind them that they have five minutes left to finish playing or tell them that after this TV cartoon it is time for bed. By preparing the children and working with, rather than against, other environmental events the mother is more likely to have her children's cooperation, and less likely to be greeted with protests and arguments. How children behave in similar situations in future will depend upon the consequences of their behaviour.

The consequences of behaviour

According to the behavioural model, the events which follow a behaviour are essential in determining whether the behaviour will be strengthened and maintained. Consequences which we find pleasant or desirable increase the likelihood that the behaviour will occur again. They can therefore strengthen or *reinforce* behaviour. Consequences which we find unpleasant or undesirable decrease the likelihood that the behaviour will be repeated. They weaken it. Behaviour can also be weakened when it is no longer followed by any pleasant or desirable consequences which previously occurred. We learn to behave in ways which have desirable consequences for us and to avoid behaving in ways which have undesirable outcomes. By strengthening some behaviours and weakening others, the consequences serve to shape the pattern of our behaviour over a period of time and in different settings.

Many of the consequences for children's behaviour in class are provided by the teacher. By understanding and using these appropriately the teacher can therefore strengthen behaviours that he wishes to see in class and weaken behaviours that he considers undesirable or inappropriate in the classroom setting.

LEARNING THROUGH EXPERIENCE

Having explored the separate effects of setting events and consequences on behaviour, we now turn to the central question, which is '*How* do we learn to behave in the ways we do?' According to the behavioural model, the setting events and consequences provided by the environment operate together to shape our behaviour over time and in different situations.

For illustrative purposes we take a simple example of how this process works, in which a person is presented with a puzzle. In this case, the materials used provide the 'environmental' setting events and consequences. Life is not always so convenient! Nevertheless, using the behavioural model, the principles illustrated here can be applied to more complex behaviours and situations.

Imagine our adult 'learner', who finds himself presented with a 100-piece jigsaw puzzle. His previous experience of jigsaws is very limited. He is asked to put the pieces together to make a village scene. Since he is to do this alone, through direct experience, he is given no further guidance nor the help of a picture.

He is likely to begin by turning all the pieces so he can see their colour-markings and then to try and fit individual pieces together in pairs or groups according to their colour and shape. His activity is a complicated series of interactions between his behaviour and the pieces of the jigsaw. His attempts to fit pieces together meet with differing consequences. Either the pieces fit or they do not! Each of these consequences then becomes the setting event for other behaviours and the chain of events continues.

In each instance the setting events give cues which tell the learner how to behave. The consequences tell him whether his behaviour was successful or unsuccessful. They give him 'feedback' which guides his choice of pieces and the ways in which he tries to fit them together.

By repeating this process many times he begins to discriminate among the shapes and colours of the pieces more selectively. He is learning by the outcomes of his behaviour which pieces to try together and which to leave. He may, with increasing experience, learn strategies which heighten his chances of success. For example, he may seek all those pieces with flat edges with which to build the border, and he may group pieces together by their colour markings.

The general pattern of successes and failures in fitting pieces together will not only determine what he learns to do but will also influence the likelihood that he will continue working at the jigsaw.

The more unsuccessful attempts he has, the more likely that he will stop working, at least for the time being: his behaviour will be weakened by failures. However, the more *successes* he has, the more likely that his behaviour will be strengthened and he will continue to try. Of course, whether or not he successfully completes this puzzle will be a strong influence on his willingness to try others in future!

This process of learning can be applied to more complex behaviours: for example, to explain the process by which a teacher learns, through personal experience, the most effective ways of managing children in school. Thus, by trying various approaches and techniques in different situations and with different groups of pupils, she receives feedback as to which of these succeeds or fails in bringing about the desired outcome. In time she improves upon those methods which went some way to achieving the results she wanted. Her behaviour in managing her class is shaped by her direct experience in real classroom situations.

Learning alone through direct experience requires very many repetitions of relevant learning opportunities and takes time. Indeed, if left to learn alone, many useful behaviours would never be learned. Fortunately, we are rarely in a position where we must learn alone entirely through our own experience. We can and do learn from others' experience and, both as children and adults, we are helped by others to learn. The child learning to say her first words copies examples that other people deliberately give her. The teacher is given advice by, and opportunities to watch, others who are more experienced in managing class groups. In normal circumstances, even our poor jigsaw learner could expect some help, if only a picture which showed what the completed jigsaw would look like!

Other people provide us with *setting events* which show us what to do. We can imitate their demonstration, follow their spoken and written instructions, act in accordance with rules and apply principles. In all these cases we are helped to behave in ways which are likely to be appropriate in the circumstances and therefore to have desirable outcomes. In this way, too, we learn entirely new behaviours which we have not previously shown. Other people also help us to learn by providing many of the *consequences* for our behaviour.

It is unlikely that any model can be used to explain satisfactorily every aspect of human behaviour and in adopting the behavioural model we must accept that there are limitations to its application.

The model is only concerned with 'external' observable events. To say this is not to deny, in any way whatsoever, either the existence of 'non-observable' factors or that they may influence behaviour. However, they are not considered directly within the parameters of the behavioural approach.

The behavioural model has been found to be very powerful in its application to behaviour management and behaviour change, and this leads us to a further point which must be made at the outset. If we apply a powerful model to direct deliberately the learning of pupils and to encourage certain behaviours whilst restricting others, we must always be aware that there are serious ethical considerations. These will include concerns about the *measures* used in any systematic management of children's behaviour and also concerns about the *choice* of those behaviours which are required from the children.

There is a fear that the measures used in a systematic approach may be coercive or predominantly punitive. Alternatively it may be held that a systematic and 'scientific' approach to management may be cold and clinical, with little room for spontaneity or natural human relationships. We hope to dispel these concerns by demonstrating that the application of the behavioural model need not and should not carry such implications. Indeed we shall argue that the model provides the basis for a positive system of classroom management which enhances, rather than detracts from, the development of positive relationships and a pleasant atmosphere in class.

A number of issues surround the choice of behaviours which children will be taught. Who should decide which social and educational behaviours are desirable? How far should we make these decisions for children? To what extent should or could a child be involved in making these decisions for himself? What reasons underlie our choices about those behaviours which are required from children? In whose interests are these choices made? Do the desired behaviours enhance the interests of the child, the interests of the adults who work with him, or perhaps simply the child's conformity within the school system? Where there is a conflict of interests, whose should be given priority? These issues, together with those concerning the measures to be used, are discussed by McIntire (1974) and by Sulzer-Azaroff and Mayer (1977). They offer guidance on ethical safeguards which should be provided when applying the behavioural model with children, and our book assumes the provision of such safeguards.

SUMMARY

In this chapter we have considered the interrelationship between behaviour and environment. According to the behavioural model behaviour is learned: the key to this learning process being the sequence 'setting events — behaviour — consequences'.

Environmental setting events predispose us to behave in certain ways and the consequences influence the likelihood of the behaviour being repeated. Learning is a continuous process in which new behaviours are incorporated into our repertoire and are retained so long as they are reinforced in the context of particular environments. The behaviours which are reinforced alter as the surroundings and other people's behaviour towards us change. Behaviours which are no longer reinforced are then dropped from the range that we show. They may remain unused for so long that they are forgotten and in some instances may need to be relearned. It is in these ways that our patterns of behaviour are shaped by environmental influence and evolve over time.

The behavioural model offers you a conceptual framework within which you can marshal and make sense of your own experience with children in class. It offers ways of dealing with classroom situations which centre on describing observable events, rather than upon personal interpretations of these. The use of behavioural terms frees a teacher to clarify her expectations about children's performance and social behaviour. She can then communicate her expectations more clearly to her pupils, rather than using vague terms which are open to misunderstanding and confusion. The use of behavioural descriptions enables a teacher to see clearly whether children have or have not reached expectations and to offer them constructive help and feedback about what they have done. Taking the behavioural view, her verbal and written communication with others (parents and colleagues) can also be factual and clear. By keeping herself strictly to descriptions of the child's behaviour and performance even when these cause concern, she can attempt to avoid the problems which so often follow if we begin interpreting behaviour and end up labelling the child!

2

A Framework for Management

INTRODUCTION

The behavioural model focuses our attention upon the classroom and its events as an environment which is specifically designed to help children learn. Moreover it is the one which the teacher influences directly. She takes decisions about curriculum content and the related activities which she and her pupils will undertake. She arranges the room, its furniture and materials accordingly. Most importantly, she then behaves towards her pupils in certain ways and asks certain behaviours from them. In behavioural terms, she manages the setting events and consequences from which children learn.

Key points in this chapter are:

(1) When carefully planned and prepared, the classroom and events within it work with the teacher to 'set the scene' for children's appropriate behaviour.

(2) A focus on correcting misbehaviour is likely to have the opposite effect to that intended: it can led to an *increase* in misbehaviour and the time spent dealing with it.

(3) When a teacher concentrates on noticing children's appropriate behaviour and providing pleasant consequences for it, children are more likely to behave in the ways desired.

(4) To be effective, a teacher's management must be consistent over time and with different pupils.

(5) The positive and systematic management of setting events and consequences offers teachers a comprehensive framework for the management of children's behaviour in class.

THE CLASSROOM ENVIRONMENT

The effects of different environmental factors may not be easy to disentangle within a busy classroom. However we can view the environment as comprising three components: physical, social and educational. By separating these out, the teacher can organise and manage each so that together they provide for effective management of children's learning and behaviour in class.

The physical component

This is provided by the surroundings in which children and teacher are working. For the most part these are the surroundings of the classroom itself. Its basic design may vary from the 'old-fashioned' schoolroom of the late nineteenth century to the open-plan base of more modern schools. The space within the room may be arranged in different ways to provide areas for specific activities such as a 'wet' area or a book corner. In the open-plan setting these different spaces may be clearly defined, having their own enclosing walls, curtains or doors. In the more traditional rectangular room a teacher might create different areas by judicious arrangement of cupboards and carpeting. Each classroom has its assortment of furniture, materials and equipment. Some pieces are to be shared by the children, others are for individual use, still others are restricted to use only by the teacher. Of course not all the time is spent in these surroundings, for certain curricular activities require different settings and the use of specialised equipment. The principles which we shall outline will apply wherever teaching occurs. However, most of our examples are drawn from the environment of the classroom itself. Research studies (Glynn, 1982) have highlighted important ways in which the physical surroundings can influence children's behaviour, both directly and through the effects the surroundings have on the behaviour of other people working within them.

The social component

This aspect of the environment is provided by the children and teachers who gather within these surroundings. Any combination of children and teachers provides a social component which is in some respects different from any other. A teacher will work with different groups (large and small, mixed ability or 'sets') and with individuals within the larger group. At times and particularly in the open-plan situation, teachers may work as a team, sharing responsibility for the learning of perhaps an entire school year group. Whatever its size or the activity in which it is engaged, a teaching group is a collection of individuals who bring different experiences to the situation. The dynamics of these group situations will therefore always differ from one another. Nevertheless there are general principles that can be applied to the group context so that, when managed effectively, the whole group functions cohesively. Teaching objectives are best served when teacher and pupils are cooperating towards a common purpose. One main purpose is, of course, the children's efficient learning of educational tasks, and the physical and social components of the classroom are organised in such a way as to facilitate this.

The educational component

This derives from the content of the school's curricula, and from decisions which teachers take as to what skills and information children need to be taught at particular ages and stages in their learning. The tasks on which children are engaged, the organisation and presentation of these, and the patterning of activities across the school day are all key features of the educational component.

MANAGING CLASSROOM SETTING EVENTS

When we are teaching new ways of behaving, particularly educational skills, we do not usually expect children to discover and use the new skills entirely alone, for we may have to wait a long time! We deliberately set up our materials, explanations and help in such a way that, from the outset, pupils have every chance of displaying the behaviours that we wish them to learn. That is, when planning our teaching of new educational skills our first concern is the management of setting events for the children's behaviour.

This idea of setting up the situation so as to help pupils respond with appropriate behaviour from the outset is perhaps less familiar when dealing with behaviours which are not strictly 'educational'. When dealing with 'social behaviours', such as how children interact with their teachers and with one another, it is more usual to use their behaviour as the starting point and to concentrate on ways in which we can respond in order to encourage or correct what the children do. That is, there is more often a tendency to manage social behaviour by using the consequences of children's behaviour. However, factors within the physical, social and educational components of the classroom environment all provide cues which may predispose the children to behave in particular ways. Some of these are listed in Table 2.1.

Each of these factors within the classroom environment contributes to the group of setting events which may cue children's behaviour. It is important to note that they may combine to cue either behaviours which are desired by the teacher, or behaviours which the teacher does *not* want to see in these particular circumstances. The following examples illustrate how setting events can influence whether or not desired behaviour occurs.

Table 2.1: Some environmental factors which set the scene for classroom behaviours

Physical factors	Social factors	Educational factors
Amount of space for working and movement	Group sizes and composition	The type of educational task, its relevance, difficulty and length
Seating arrangement	How children are to work: together/alone etc.	Teacher's presentation and instructions.
Distribution of materials	Classroom rules Teacher's behaviour towards individuals and groups	Written instructions and examples
Noise levels	Children's behaviour towards each other and teacher	The pattern of activities across the lesson and the day

Ms Parker wants the children to start work as soon as they return to class after break

Setting 1

The bell rings and children start to walk towards their classrooms. Ms Parker is standing outside the doorway talking to John about his new baby sister. Sally and her two friends follow their classmates into the classroom. The room is arranged in five groups of tables, six seats around each. Ms Parker has collected the materials together for the next lesson, and the worksheets and boxes of pencils are on her desk. Some children are sitting at their places, others are standing around the tables talking. Three are standing at Ms Parker's desk arguing about who was asked to give out the worksheets. Given these cues, what are Sally and her friends likely to do? They may join a group or sit in their places and talk with neighbours. They may join in the argument at the desk. However, they are unlikely to sit down and start working.

Setting 2

The bell rings and children start to walk towards their classrooms. Ms Parker is standing just outside the doorway and greets the children as they pass, telling them to sit in their places and start work on their number worksheets. The room is arranged in five groups of tables, six seats around each. Named worksheets and a box of pencils are placed on each group of tables. Other children are taking their places. Given these cues, what are Sally and her friends likely to do? All the cues are pointing to the same behaviours: to sit in your place and start work. The room is arranged for this; the other children's behaviour confirms the message from the other sources (room and teacher).

In both these examples Sally and friends are behaving in a manner which is entirely consistent with the setting events. Setting 1 illustrates the point that unwanted behaviours are more likely to occur when setting events are unplanned. Ms Parker allowed the conversation with John to continue. Her instructions about who was to give out materials were unclear. As a result the behaviours cued by the setting events were not those she intended. Setting 2 illustrates that setting events can be planned and prepared so as to cue the behaviours which the teacher wishes children to show in particular circumstances. The cues provided by different factors within the environment were planned so as to confirm, rather than contradict each other.

Setting events are as relevant to social as to academic behaviour. Through her planning of lessons and the decisions she takes about which skills individuals and groups of pupils should be taught next, the teacher determines the basis from which all setting events will follow. The tasks chosen, the pattern of activities across the day and the presentation of these, the organisation of the classroom and materials will not only set the occasion for children's academic behaviour. They will also influence the ways in which pupils behave in relation to their teacher, tasks and one another.

The systematic management of setting events also has implications for children's future learning. The more that we can help the children to respond appropriately and consistently to the cues provided by their learning tasks and situations in class, the more likely it is that they will continue to do so when they encounter other, similar tasks and situations in future. The effective use of setting events is therefore as important to the children's ability to generalise their behaviours beyond the immediate situation as it is to their learning of new skills and the behaviours which are appropriate in the here-and-now of the classroom.

Setting events do not by themselves teach children. It is not enough to provide demonstrations, clear instructions and interesting activities. Nor is it sufficient only to plan the classroom so that all aspects of the environment encourage the behaviours which are desired. Children will not learn merely by watching someone else or by hearing about the best way to do something. They will learn by doing and by experiencing the consequences of their actions. Nevertheless, if we may use the cart and horse analogy, we would view the management of classroom setting events as the horse, whilst behaviour and its consequences would be placed as the cart. If the horse is led in the right direction, then the cart is likely to follow; and it is far easier to control direction by working on the horse than the cart! Hence our emphasis throughout is on the setting events as the starting point for all aspects of classroom management.

MANAGING CLASSROOM CONSEQUENCES

The behavioural model offers you, as teacher, a choice in your management of consequences for children's performance and classroom behaviours. The option you choose depends on whether you direct your efforts towards behaviours you want to see, or towards those which you do not.

A teacher could work to increase those behaviours which he wants his pupils to show: improvement in their academic performance and 'good' behaviour in class. For example, he might make effective use of his own approval, stars and other types of reward to encourage the children to behave well, try hard and achieve in their work. Alternatively, he could work to decrease those behaviours which are not wanted, correcting the children's mistakes and discouraging 'troublesome' behaviour. For example, he might point out the errors in their work and help individuals to make corrections. He may criticise work which is far below an individual's usual standard and ask the child to repeat the task. He may use reminders, his disapproval and a range of sanctions to discourage misbehaviour.

Many teachers may feel they use a mixture of the positive and corrective approaches in their management, depending on how well they expect the children to succeed at what is asked of them. For example, they may use the positive approach when educational tasks or classroom routines are new to the children: but use a corrective one once they judge that pupils have had sufficient experience, or have shown the correct behaviour on some occasions and therefore can be expected to do so again.

The positive alternative may be more usual in managing children's behaviour on their academic tasks but the corrective pattern more common in dealing with social behaviour (Wheldall and Merrett, 1984a). These differences in approach may well reflect those in a teacher's expectations. Thus we cannot expect children to succeed immediately and show perfect performance on academic activities. In this area then, we are perhaps likely to be more encouraging in our approach. However, there is perhaps an expectation that children can, and should, behave well in class. It then follows that they are reprimanded when they do not!

The tendency to adopt a corrective, rather than a positive pattern of consequences in the management of social behaviour may also reflect the concern caused to teachers by the 'troublesome' behaviours which children show in class. British primary teachers who took part in a survey (Merrett and Wheldall, 1978) nominated 'talking out of turn' as the most common troublesome behaviour, with 'non-attending', 'disobeying' and 'disturbing others' ranked close behind. Every teacher could update this list, replacing or adding misbehaviours which they notice in their classrooms. They may share the concern expressed by 62 per cent of teachers in the survey that they spent more time dealing with order and control problems than they felt they ought to. There is little doubt that unwanted behaviours are a cause for concern among primary teachers as well as among their colleagues in secondary schools.

Thus expectations and concerns about children's behaviour can naturally lead to a focus on undesired behaviour and ways in which it can be weakened and reduced: that is, to a corrective pattern of management, at least for social behaviour. We shall therefore discuss this option first, with its implications for teacher and pupils.

Using consequences in a corrective pattern

This orientation involves the teacher being alert to behaviour which is unacceptable or troublesome and acting on this directly. For example, the teacher may tell children to 'Sit down', 'Turn around' or 'Be quiet', and remind them when they are doing other than she wishes. The teacher's intention is that, in time, children will stop behaving in troublesome ways and that they will be left showing only behaviour which is acceptable or desired in class. In this case acceptable behaviour is defined as the absence of unwanted behaviour.

The teacher might use a variety of consequences (corrections, reminders, reprimands) for undesired behaviour. If it persists she may warn children that free play, preferred activities or perhaps house points are likely to be withdrawn. It is intended that as a result children will learn to get on with their work. Particularly 'good' behaviour or performance may be noticed and recognised by praise, house points or other pleasant or valued outcomes. By definition, however, these instances will be more the exception than the rule.

Implications of a corrective pattern

At first sight this approach looks to be effective. Children sit down and get on with their work when told, and it seems that troublesome behaviour occurs less often. Initially the teacher may be encouraged and may expect to spend less time dealing with misbehaviour, so that she can devote her attention to helping the children with their work.

However in practice a corrective approach can result in the teacher spending more, rather than less, time dealing with unwanted behaviour. Studies have shown that the general use of consequences to correct unwanted behaviour is likely to result in outcomes opposite to those intended: that is, to an *increase* in children's misbehaviour and a corresponding increase in teacher time spent dealing with it. There are two fundamental problems with the approach, which centre on what the children and their teacher learn as a result of corrective management.

What the children learn

You will recognise that when a teacher reminds, corrects or

22

reprimands children for misbehaviour he is also giving them his attention. Now many children like adult attention and so are likely to repeat behaviour which gets them noticed by their teacher. Therefore, whilst the teacher intends to discourage misbehaviour, he may in effect be strengthening it by giving his attention! This is known as the *'criticism trap'* and is the first problem with a corrective pattern of management.

Becker, Engelmann and Thomas (1975) describe an elegant observational study of this phenomenon and its effects in class. The number of times children were told by their teachers to 'Sit down' when they were standing was deliberately varied over a period of weeks. It was found that the more often the teachers told pupils to 'Sit down', the more often children stood up. Giving teacher attention in this way actually served to reinforce or strengthen standing up by the children. Telling them to sit down was therefore teaching them to stand up! 'Sit down' was also acting as a setting event which cued the desired behaviour, since children did sit down when told. This would give the impression that telling them to sit down was working. Becker, Engelmann and Thomas (1975, p. 68) concluded:

> *A Beautiful Trap!* Imagine, the teacher thought that telling the children to sit down worked, because they *did sit down*. But that was only the immediate effect. The effect on standing might have been missed altogether by the teacher if careful observations had not been made. Her words were in fact having exactly the opposite effect on standing from what she desired.

Other studies (McNaughton, 1981; McNaughton and Glynn, 1981) have illustrated how similar effects can occur in relation to children's errors when they are reading to a teacher who immediately intervenes when errors are made. The effects of the criticism trap can be expected to occur when teacher attention, praise and other pleasant consequences for appropriate and desired behaviours are uncommon.

This point directs us to the second problem with the corrective pattern of management. The busy teacher, who is alert to mistakes and misbehaviour and concentrates upon dealing with these as and when they occur, is likely to overlook behaviour which is merely satisfactory. She is less likely to comment when children are getting on quietly with their work than when they are not. Similarly, she is less likely to comment upon a child's performance unless it is noticeably different from his usual standard. However, behaviours that go unnoticed or are ignored are likely to eventually die out; this process is known as 'extinction' (see Chapter 9). The teacher who generally uses consequences in a corrective pattern may therefore unintentionally weaken the very behaviours she wants to see by failing to observe and comment on them.

Thus a focus on undesired behaviour can have the opposite effect on children's learning from that which is intended: the criticism trap has the effect that the children learn to misbehave whilst their acceptable behaviours go without the teacher's attention and are subsequently weakened.

What the teacher learns

We have seen that when a teacher corrects or nags the children, they are likely to do as they are told — for the moment. The misbehaviour stops and, as this is desired by the teacher, her correcting, criticising and disapproval are strengthened. Therefore she is likely to behave in these ways more often. Whatever her initial intentions may have been, the teacher learns to nag, criticise and disapprove.

Sadly, this vicious circle in which the teacher learns to correct and the children learn to misbehave can lead a harassed and worried teacher into increasing difficulties of class control. She may frequently find herself using more reprimands and threats, and removing privileges. She may refer children more often to 'higher authorities' in school for correction and end up employing reprimands with the whole class or with individuals who have not really deserved them.

At the least then, a corrective pattern of consequences for children's behaviour can result in more misbehaviours and in more teacher time spent correcting them. At worst, it can lead to a negative classroom atmosphere in which teacher and pupils are set apart so that their mutual cooperation towards the goal of teaching and learning is lost. It is because of the dangers associated with the use of this approach that we would not consider this option appropriate to the management of either children's academic or social behaviour.

Using consequences in a positive pattern

This approach to the management of consequences involves a teacher being alert to desired classroom behaviour and to improved performance and acting upon them directly. The teacher 'catches' the children when they behave acceptably, shows he is pleased and tells them what it is they are doing that is 'good'. He will use his own attention and praise as consequences for appropriate behaviour, together with perhaps points or stars. He probably also allows the children to move on to more popular activities once less preferred or more tedious tasks are completed. The intention here is that appropriate behaviours are in this way strengthened and will occur more often. That is, the children will learn to behave well and to work hard in class. As they learn to behave well and to work hard the incompatible misbehaviours will occur less often. For example, if they learn to stay in their seats during certain activities they cannot also be standing or walking away from their places!

Implications of a positive pattern

This approach has the intrinsic appeal for any pleasant scene. Imagine, the teacher moves around the room giving encouragement here and gentle praise there; the children work enthusiastically, enjoying their teacher's praise and the surety that he will help and encourage; their 'hard' work completed, they then move on to more entertaining and lively learning activities at the end of the session . . . If only it were that easy!

In fact, it does not always seem natural to praise and to be encouraging; rather it is more natural to leave things alone when they are going smoothly and to take direct action only when they go wrong. It therefore takes effort and practice first of all to notice acceptable performance and behaviour and then to overcome the tendency to dismiss it as, 'Only what I expect to see anyway'. Furthermore, it may feel awkward or embarrassing to use praise and other rewards liberally. There is a tendency to reserve these for unusually successful performance or particularly improved behaviour. To use them for the ordinary may seem somehow false or even wasteful, carrying the concern that their effects may be reduced through overuse. Moreover, it is difficult to behave positively when one is weary, unwell or feeling irritated by events. Therefore, to use consequences consistently in a positive pattern requires that the teacher works hard to overcome these effects and quite literally to 'keep smiling'.

Other difficulties which are often cited in translating this management approach into practice centre on the fact that misbehaviours will not be entirely eliminated. Their occurrence, and how the teacher should respond to them, is a natural cause for concern. The temptation is to act upon all undesired behaviours directly so that it may be clear to the children that these are not acceptable. One advantage of the positive approach is that, when the focus is upon appropriate behaviour, the teacher is alert to those behaviours which are desired rather than to those harmless but irritating unwanted behaviours that might otherwise catch her notice. Without adult attention such minor misdemeanours are likely to gradually fade and disappear (see Chapter 9). The teacher who uses consequences positively treats misbehaviours of this kind as the cue for her to give attention to children who are showing the desired behaviour. In this way the teacher is consistently directing her own attention and that of the children towards appropriate behaviours, and weakening those which are unwanted.

The adoption of a positive pattern of management does not exclude the word 'No' from a teacher's vocabulary. Nor does it preclude the use of correction and discouragement. The effect of the criticism trap will not be found when attention is occasionally given to unwanted behaviour but always in the context of *frequent* attention for desired behaviour. There are some misbehaviours which, because of their effects on learning, relationships or safety, cause a teacher concern and need to be eliminated quickly. It is to this minority of unwanted behaviours that the use of stronger corrective measures is restricted (see Chapter 9).

Of course prevention is always preferable to cure and alternatives to corrective measures must therefore always be sought: for example, teaching an alternative, acceptable behaviour which is incompatible with the misbehaviour, closely supervising children's contact with any potentially harmful equipment, etc.

An effective pattern of management includes, of course, the management of consequences provided by sources other than the teacher: the children's work and the children themselves. Some activities have built-in consequences which tell a child whether his attempts at the task were correct. On many other tasks the child must rely on the teacher to provide information on whether his work is correct, particularly in the early stages of learning. This knowledge of results, or 'feedback', is fundamental to the learning of new skills. It is also widely recognised (Johnson and Johnson, 1975; Vargas, 1977; Clarizio, 1980) that *success* in learning tasks is crucial to children's subsequent learning and to their behaviour in class. It is therefore essential that a positive pattern of consequences is used as systematically in the teacher's management of children's *learning* as it is in the management of their *behaviour*.

The behaviour of other children in the group is a source of both pleasant and unpleasant consequences for a child's behaviour. They may answer a classmate, laugh, clap, hit him back and so on. When the teacher uses consequences in a positive way for desired behaviour, it is more likely that, as a group of individuals, the children will behave in ways which are wanted by their teacher. In this case we could anticipate that the consequences children provide for each other will be compatible with those from the teacher. Difficulties may arise when misbehaviours which the teacher would ignore or discourage are given attention by classmates and are thereby strengthened. However, a positive pattern of management can be applied on a group as well as an individual basis. For example, the whole group could earn points which allow access to free choice activities at the end of a work period if *everyone* is keeping the rules when the teacher checks during the session. This will lead the children to relate to one another in a manner similar to that of the teacher (see Chapter 9).

The advantages of a positive approach to the use of consequences are many and centre on what the children (and their teacher) learn from their experiences in class. The teacher works directly on the behaviour and performance she wishes to see — the ordinary, as well as the particularly good.

What the children learn

When a teacher carefully chooses the pleasant consequences she intends to provide for appropriate behaviours, and uses them systematically, these behaviours will occur more often. The children learn to behave in desired ways. If at the same time incompatible minor misbehaviours are not given attention, they will be weakened and occur less often. There will still be limits to what the children *can* do in class, and serious misbehaviour can be acted upon directly by restricted and cautious use of procedures which interrupt and correct the behaviour. However, the teacher is always working to draw the children's attention to their appropriate behaviour rather than telling them when their behaviour is unacceptable. Furthermore, the children are given opportunities to learn how to encourage and praise, by following their teacher's example in her behaviour towards them!

What the teacher learns

Becker, Engelmann and Thomas (1975) describe what happened when a teacher effectively changed her pattern of management to

27

one in which she consistently praised the children for working and ignored them when they were not. The results of detailed observations in the classroom led to the conclusion:

> It took some time for the teacher to become comfortable in her new role . . . but the children responded to her new behaviour whether she felt comfortable about it or not. The classroom became quieter; many members learned to work on-task for long periods of time. There was order and co-operation. The teacher found she had more time to teach now that she spent less time trying to control the children.
>
> (Becker, Engelmann and Thomas, 1975, p. 54)

There were desirable outcomes for this teacher in terms of the children's behaviour and her increased opportunities to teach them, rather than control their behaviour. Thus not only the children were learning here; their teacher was learning a positive and effective pattern of management. Other examples of the use of this approach, with desired outcomes for the teachers concerned, are described elsewhere (Wheldall and Merrett, 1984b).

At the least then, a positive pattern of consequences in class can improve the children's behaviour and reduce teacher time spent dealing with misbehaviour. At best it can lead to a positive classroom atmosphere in which teacher and pupils work together towards joint objectives: effective teaching and efficient learning. Of the two options offered by the behavioural model it is therefore this pattern of consequence management that we choose for both academic and social behaviour.

GETTING THE RIGHT CONSISTENCY

So far in this chapter we have treated the management of setting events and consequences separately. Does this mean that the behavioural model leads us to two distinct strategies which can be used interchangeably, together, or in part? The short answer is No! Neither strategy can be used to maximum effect if used partially or in isolation. There must be consistency throughout your management if your pupils are to make sense of their classroom environment and learn effectively from their experiences.

Consistency in the management of setting events and consequences

Behaviours are often more appropriate in certain situations than in others and this will affect the consequences which follow them. Consequences confirm the behaviour as appropriate or inappropriate in the context of the particular circumstances in which it took place. Thus the consequences not only influence the likelihood that a behaviour will be repeated, but also the circumstances in which it is likely to recur. Through this association the consequences increase the control which setting events have over behaviour. They increase the likelihood that particular situations will cue certain behaviours.

For the learning of appropriate behaviours to take place quickly and efficiently it is therefore important to ensure consistency between setting events and consequences.

Consistency over time and with different pupils

If the teacher is to enable children to make sense of their environment, to learn new behaviours readily and to maintain them, it is crucial that his classroom management is consistent from day to day and from week to week. Clearly if a child completes the same task in the same way but on one day receives praise from his teacher and on another correction, then he will be confused as to what is wanted. Where this happens often, a pupil may also learn to mistrust his teacher!

The teacher must also ensure that persistent minor unwanted behaviours to which she is tempted to give her attention are weakened instead, by ignoring them over a period of time. If the teacher ignores an irritating behaviour on most days, but attends to it occasionally, she may unwittingly be maintaining and even strengthening the very behaviour she wishes to weaken. For intermittent attention is known to be a powerful way of sustaining behaviour which is already well established!

Of course children not only learn by events which happen to them but by watching other people in their environment. It is therefore crucial that behaviour is treated in a consistent manner, regardless of *who* behaved in that way. The teacher must achieve this consistency in her management of the class group for several reasons. By giving credit wherever it is due, she is fair and is *seen to be* fair, thereby enlisting the children's support and trust. She is providing clear messages for the children as to which behaviours are wanted. She is pointing out examples of the behaviour which she wishes to see, rather than holding up individual pupils as examples for the rest.

For these reasons consistency is also essential in the use of all procedures for dealing with unwanted behaviours. Again the message should be clear: it is the behaviour which is unacceptable, rather than the child himself. The axiom here is 'Give credit where it is due and don't bend the rules'.

A POSITIVE SYSTEM OF MANAGEMENT

The behavioural model's analysis of the effects of environment on behaviour offers you a comprehensive framework for classroom management, of which the management of setting events and consequences are two integral parts. You can consistently manage the classroom and events within it to show the children what is wanted, to maximise their chances of performing educational tasks successfully and behaving in ways which are appropriate. Then using a positive pattern of consequences in which the focus is upon desirable behaviours and providing pleasant consequences for them, you can confirm and strengthen these behaviours. You make it more likely that your pupils will continue to keep trying, make progress and behave acceptably in class. (See Table 2.2)

Although designed with the intention of assisting a teacher to help children learn more efficiently, a positive system of management offers wider benefits — for both children and teacher alike. Its orientation involves setting up the classroom situation systematically and consistently so that children are more likely to 'get it right' and receive pleasant outcomes for doing so. They have frequent

Table 2.2: Key features of a positive system of management

(1) Concentrate on the positive
(2) Use the classroom and events to show children how to behave
(3) Be willing to acknowledge desired behaviour and performance even when it is only what you expect anyway
(4) When dealing with unwanted behaviour is it the *behaviour* that is unacceptable, not the child.
(5) Be consistent over time and with different children

opportunities to *use* the skills, concepts and principles which they are learning. They use them in situations which are geared towards success and encouragement, rather than risking failure and discouragement. A positive system of management therefore enables the teacher to create a positive classroom atmosphere in which desired and appropriate behaviours are strengthened and occur more often. Mutual cooperation between teacher and learners is sustained and a pattern of success in learning tasks is established. As a result of past successes the work itself becomes rewarding for the children so that they are likely to generalise good work habits and an interest in learning to other settings beyond the classroom, and independent of the presence of one particular teacher.

SUMMARY

In this chapter we discussed the application of a behavioural approach to a teacher's management of children's behaviour.

First we explored the management of setting events provided by physical, social and educational aspects of the classroom environment. These can be arranged so that they work with the teacher, to maximise children's chances of behaving in desired ways.

Then we considered the consequences a teacher might provide for children's behaviour. A focus on correcting misbehaviour and mistakes is likely to have the opposite effect to that intended by the teacher. This pattern of consequence management can lead to an *increase* in unwanted behaviour and the time spent dealing with it.

We therefore advocated the alternative, which involves focusing on children's appropriate behaviour and working on this directly by providing pleasant consequences which strengthen and maintain it. This approach to consequence management does accommodate the need to sometimes deal directly, and effectively, with unwanted behaviour. However, it is an essentially positive approach, with benefits for pupils and teacher alike.

We have stressed the need for consistency in a teacher's management over time and with different pupils. The positive and consistent management of classroom setting events and consequences offers teachers a comprehensive framework for classroom management: *a positive system of management.*

In the next and final chapter of Part One we explore the implications of this behavioural approach for certain aspects of the teaching role. In Parts Two and Three we go on to outline ways in which a positive management system can be applied to the day-to-day management of children's behaviour in class.

3

A Framework for Teaching

INTRODUCTION

The behavioural model offers teachers a conceptual framework which goes well beyond providing a practical approach to the management of children's behaviour. Its concern with observable events and its particular view of learning and teaching have clear implications for the teaching role. In this final chapter of Part One we consider five aspects of the teaching role from a behavioural view point: deciding what to teach, classroom organisation, working with the children, evaluating progress and communicating information.

The teacher acts as an agent of change. She takes decisions on what to teach and how to teach it. She arranges the classroom environment in ways which enable children to learn more quickly and effectively than they would do alone. She also creates a positive classroom atmosphere which promotes successful learning. She carefully observes the progress her pupils make and judges the outcomes of her teaching in terms of what the children learn. Throughout her work a teacher is communicating with other people: her pupils, their parents and her colleagues.

DECIDING WHAT TO TEACH

Over time a school will evolve curricula to teach basic literacy and numeracy skills as well as subjects such as art, drama, environmental studies, etc. These curricula form the basis of what is taught and decisions are made to select a range of appropriate activities for all the pupils in the class. The tasks described in the various curricula reflect the overall aims and goals that a school has for its pupils. These will, in general, relate to the skills, attitudes and experiences it is thought children will need in order to develop independence and lead fulfilling lives during, and after they have left, school.

Within this framework a teacher takes decisions about what to teach particular groups and individuals over the coming weeks and days. The learning activities she plans will depend upon what, exactly, children have already learned and which behaviours they need to learn. Such 'needs' have been defined by Vargas (1977) as 'behaviours which a person lacks which are necessary to function effectively and independently both in the present and in the future' (p. 212).

Each class group is a collection of individuals who will already have learned different skills to varying levels of competence as a result of their previous experiences in and out of school. Therefore at the beginning of the year and throughout its course, the teacher must find out what all members of the class group have already learned in order to establish which behaviours to teach and which of these should have priority.

Since, from a behavioural point of view there can be no teaching without learning, a teacher cannot assume that because certain skills and information have been 'covered' last year or last week they have *therefore* been taught. They must also be seen to have been learned. Only by seeing what children can *do* at any point can the teacher be sure what has been learned and take decisions as to what should be taught next. Using a behavioural approach then, a teacher will, as far as possible, define his teaching objectives in terms of what children should be able to do as a result of effective teaching (Mager, 1962; Gronlund, 1970; McIntire, 1974; Ainscow and Tweddle, 1979).

To be really specific and clear to all, teaching objectives need to include not only what the pupil can do to demonstrate that a skill has been learned, but also to what standard of performance. Objectives can then be expressed to the pupils in such a way that they know at the outset what is expected of them and what are the important features of the task. For example, supposing children are set a written task: to write a story. The important features of the task may be that they write a story that has a beginning, a middle, and an ending. Particular features of punctuation or of spelling may have diminished importance in this task. It is important that the children know at the outset which are the important features, rather than be told on presenting a carefully punctuated piece of work that 'Its fine as far as it goes, but it doesn't have an ending'.

Specifying teaching objectives in terms of what children can *do as a result of* their learning and to what *level of competence* carries many advantages for teacher and pupils alike. Expressing objectives in this way helps a teacher to plan the children's learning experiences, to pinpoint what each child needs to learn and to track their progress. This in turn helps the teacher to see when children are not learning efficiently or quickly enough and to plan extra help when needed. Children are involved in their learning from the start, since what they do is the important feature throughout. They can be clear about what is expected of them and can be directed towards, and concentrate upon, what are the important features of a given task. Finally the children will themselves be able to see the evidence of their own progress in meeting the objectives which are set, and that their teacher is helping them to learn.

CLASSROOM ORGANISATION

We see the teaching environment as comprising three components: physical, social and educational. As we have indicated, teaching intentions will be conveyed to pupils by the way the total environment is organised. So each component needs to be well planned and managed in a way that enables teachers to communicate effectively with their pupils.

There have probably been occasions when you have watched a colleague teaching and been impressed by the way in which every aspect of the classroom environment was geared to teaching and learning. The atmosphere existing between teacher and pupils was positive and lessons were well-organised, with children working on appropriate tasks. It is important to bear in mind that features of an effectively run classroom can be identified by the children as well as by visiting teachers!

WORKING WITH THE CHILDREN

Having decided what to teach, and set up the classroom environment, the teacher manages children's interactions with the environment. She then evaluates outcomes in terms of what the children have learned. Children are taught a wide range of skills while at school. In the primary years there is an emphasis on teaching literacy and numeracy skills which are essential for success at secondary school level and ultimately in later life. Equally the primary school is where pupils experience their first intensive and prolonged social encounters with the outside world. There are many varied and subtle aspects to successful social interactions, some of which have been acquired by children before they attend school. Others will be learned later either through experience or through direct teaching by family, teachers and others.

Behavioural psychology provides the teacher with an analysis of the important aspects of the environment which change behaviour. Much of a teacher's success rests on appropriate advanced planning and organisation of the classroom environment, which pave the way for the daily interactions that occur between teacher and pupils. In many respects the teacher's role can be compared to that of a composer who, having written a symphony, then conducts the orchestra! The teacher arranges the classroom, identifies the needs of the children, sets appropriate academic and social objectives, and then undertakes to orchestrate all the pupils' daily activities.

For teaching to happen a teacher must operate on two fronts during contact time. First she must, through her own behaviour and the activities she presents, communicate new skills and information effectively. Secondly, she must supervise the myriad of social interactions that take place during each school day. When managed positively and consistently, pupils are more likely to relate well to their peers and teacher and feel motivated to work.

EVALUATING PROGRESS

If the teacher is to monitor children's work and evaluate progress, systematic record-keeping procedures are vital. A considerable amount of information needs to be gathered, assimilated and recalled to evaluate children's progress in response to selected teaching procedures. The human memory is fallible and cannot be expected to retain all the necessary details when making decisions about teaching approaches. Hence the essential value of an organised record-keeping system. Record-keeping requires attention to detail and a regular time commitment. The busy teacher who is concerned to prepare and conduct effective learning sessions will want a record-keeping system which places minimum demands on time and yet contains all the necessary information. It should be easy to update and be regarded as an integral part of effective classroom teaching.

Continuous records have several functions. They provide the basis for *initial assessment* of pupils' skill levels, enabling the teacher to *decide what to teach*. They help the teacher to *monitor progress* over time and to systematically observe children's improvements in response to the teaching given. This information can be used to evaluate and identify successful teaching methods and help the teacher to decide what to teach next. Alternatively, when pupils' progress is slower than we would hope, records will assist decisions about what steps can be taken to put children back on course for success. Finally, effective records assist the teacher's *communication* with other people.

There are many occasions when children can be actively involved in completing records and evaluating their own progress. They can monitor their development in learning particular skills and take part in conversations with their teacher about how they are improving.

Record-keeping systems associated with the behavioural approach collect factual information based on what teachers can see and record in the classroom. This includes details of skills the children have been taught and the ways they behave, the areas over which the teacher has direct influence. Comments about progress which are based on assumptions about children's lives outside school would, in general, be excluded. However, records might, in some circumstances, draw a teacher's attention to known details about a pupil which might affect classroom performance, such as specific medical requirements, recent family bereavement, etc.

COMMUNICATING INFORMATION

During the course of the school year, information collected about pupils may well need to be communicated to a variety of people. The success of this information exchange depends on both the quality of records kept and the thought and sensitivity with which details are related. When planning how to inform others about children it is often a good idea to place yourself in the shoes of the person you are talking to. Doing so will assist in the collection of the most suitable and relevant information and help to ensure it is presented to them in a constructive way. So bear in mind that effective communication depends on the accuracy and completeness of the information you have — and upon how you use it!

Pupils

Experiencing success acts as a powerful motivator and incentive to continue working hard. Thus, by providing frequent feedback on academic and social progress clearly and positively, the teacher will facilitate children's learning of new skills. Membership of a classroom where children are praised for the work they have done will be rewarding for pupils and teachers alike. As we have already noted, it is particularly important to tell pupils when they are achieving and behaving *acceptably*. Unfortunately this does not happen as often as perhaps it should, for reasons we have already touched upon.

A teacher needs to think how to provide feedback and communicate with children when things are going well. Thought also needs to be given to what happens when children are behaving inappropriately. As mentioned in Chapter 2, and consistent with the interpretation of teaching offered in Chapter 1, a distinction needs to be made between the child and the unwanted behaviour that child is displaying. Children need to be made aware that when an aspect of their social behaviour is considered unacceptable this is not also interpreted as a comment on them as people. It is the behaviour which is being questioned, not the pupil. Similarly when children fail to make the expected academic progress it is important to make clear to them that it is the *programme of work* which is 'failing' and not they themselves. In this case, children can be told not to worry, that amendments will need to be made in the teaching approach and that these will put the pupil back on course for success.

Parents

Schools usually arrange a regular series of parent evenings during each academic year. Most parents are naturally keen to know how their children are progressing. They will appreciate seeing evidence of improvements and being given a well-balanced picture of their child's overall development. Quite often they will be only too willing to help teach their children at home should the need arise. Various projects (White, Solity and Reeve, 1984; Topping and Wolfendale, 1985), have been reported recently of instances where parents provided effective instruction to their children, some of whom were seen to be experiencing difficulties in learning to read. What about the parents who do not come to parents' evening?

Isn't it often the case that those parents teachers most want to see do not turn up? Thoughts similar to this are frequently expressed in the staff room on the days surrounding parent evenings. It is often speculated that these parents are not interested in their children's education, that school progress is low among family priorities. While there may be some parents for whom this is true, it will certainly not always be the case. Perhaps the proposed times are inconvenient for family or financial reasons; there may be difficulties in arranging for other children to be looked after while parents visit school, etc.

Some parents who do not attend are those whose children are perceived as 'troublemakers'. Much of their contact with the school may therefore be negative, for example being called up to school to discuss incidents of bad behaviour by their child. These parents might well wish to avoid parent evenings because they may anticipate hearing little positive said about their child. Alternatively some parents may well be overawed by the thought of going up to the school. Their own school days may not have been the happiest time of their lives and they could well feel apprehensive about meetings with teachers. Perhaps they expect all teachers to be like their own and may recall them as unsympathetic or as people who used expressions and explanations that were difficult to understand. These are considerations to be borne in mind when making plans for contact with parents.

Many schools have excellent relationships with parents. Parents are always made to feel welcome when visiting these schools and may be involved in a range of school activities, regarding school as an integral part of their neighbourhood. Visits are held at convenient times and provide an opportunity for constructive dialogues between teachers and parents and also an opportunity to observe and become involved in the classroom.

A behavioural approach can help you create the general context for constructive relationships with parents. First, by helping you promote a positive classroom atmosphere and children's learning, the approach will affect what your *pupils* think and say about school! Secondly, the approach helps you to notice positive aspects of your pupils' classroom behaviour and progress — even though some aspects may sometimes give cause for concern. You will therefore be able to offer parents, as well as their children, positive and encouraging comments. Not least, a behavioural approach will help you communicate a clear and balanced view when discussing a problem or difficult situation with parents, for what you say will be

39

based more on factual information than supposition or opinion. Finally, by helping you to be clear about your pupils' progress, behaviour and needs, this approach will free you during your contacts with parents to concentrate on the *parents* and how you relate to them.

Colleagues

At the end of the school year children's records are passed on to a new teacher who usually makes time to study them and extract information which will be useful when organising work for the new term. The most constructive records for this purpose are more objective in nature, describing skills and behaviours that have been observed and relating these to the content and methods of the previous year's teaching and management. They may even contain details of exactly where children are placed on the curriculum in various subject areas and indicate which skills they need to be taught next. This is also the kind of information teachers will find most helpful when working together in a teaching or planning team, and when discussing children with colleagues during the course of the school year. School records that are sensitive to these areas will prove invaluable.

Other professionals

There may be occasions during a pupil's school career when he will come into contact with other professionals (for example, remedial teacher, doctor, speech therapist, educational psychologist, etc.) Since a class teacher works alongside children everyday in the classroom, she is an important source of information and possesses a wealth of knowledge relating to each professional's own specialist area.

For example, an educational psychologist, when consulted about a particular child, will probably request details of the child's progress in various areas of the curriculum and social behaviour in a range of situations. The speech therapist, on the other hand, will doubtless ask for information relating specifically to progress in the acquisition of receptive and expressive language skills and in the clarity of the child's speech.

The introduction of the 1981 Education Act and its related regulations in 1983 has meant that British teachers may be requested by their local education authorities (LEAs) to provide formal advice on the educational needs of certain pupils. On the basis of the formal advice reports received from three professional sources (teachers, educational psychologists and school medical officers) and representations by the child's parents, the LEA identifies a child's educational needs and determines the best provision to meet those needs. It is important to remember that the advice offered by teachers (and by any other professionals for that matter) can only be as good as the information on which it is based. Of course this is not just true when writing formal advice reports but applies equally to writing any reports about children. However, the legal procedures have highlighted the need for detailed and comprehensive information. If little is known about the skills a child has been taught, the ways in which he has been taught, his progress in relation to his peers and the relative success of different teaching approaches, then the task of advising the authority about his needs becomes particularly difficult!

A further point to bear in mind is that professional advice submitted to the authority will usually be made available to parents. It is therefore necessary in our view to be extremely conscientious in collecting classroom-based information about children, ensuring that statements made in reports are clearly written, and are factually based. If there are implications for additional resources, then the report should be sufficiently comprehensive to support the case for supplying these resources to meet a child's educational needs. Last, but by no means least, it is crucial to read the draft report *from the parent's point of view* to check that the facts are sensitively presented.

SUMMARY

In Chapter 3 we discussed the implications of the behavioural model for the teaching role.

From a behavioural viewpoint, the teacher is an agent of change. He takes decisions on what to teach based on what, exactly, pupils have already learned, what they need to learn and in what order of priority. His teaching objectives make clear what children should be able to *do* as a result of teaching and to what level of competence. The teacher than arranges the classroom environment in ways that enable children to learn more quickly and effectively than they would do alone and he creates a positive classroom atmosphere which promotes enjoyable learning.

The teacher carefully monitors children's progress and evaluates his teaching in terms of what his pupils learn. He develops comprehensive continuous records which include details of children's progress and teaching needs. Detailed and accurate records are of enormous help when a teacher is communicating information to other people: children and their parents, colleagues and other professionals.

Part Two

Setting the Scene for 'Good' Behaviour

4

The Talking Classroom

INTRODUCTION

The effects of the physical environment and the working conditions which it provides have long been of interest to industrial and commercial organisations. Working conditions, particularly those which affect the health, safety and welfare of employees, are the subject of legislation (see, for example, Ruff, 1981). Factors which contribute to the performance and satisfaction of employees, to communications and organisational effectiveness have been investigated in numerous studies, in the search for those designs and conditions which maximise the efficiency or productivity of factories, offices and other workplaces (Sundstrom, 1987).

Of course school buildings, too, constitute physical environments designed for particular purposes, and in the United Kingdom key aspects of school design, such as minimum teaching space and levels of illumination, are guided by regulations (for example, Department of Education and Science, 1972).

Clearly, ideas as to what constitutes a 'well-designed' school have changed markedly over the years in response to developments in educational practice, and to economic and social factors. However, schools are not exchanged on a 'new lamps for old' basis and, moreover, as a teacher you are very rarely in a position to exert any direct influence upon the design and working conditions of your school. Your new school will be completed and most of its contents ordered at the time of your appointment, or the school and contents may have occupied their places on the site for many years! It is natural in these circumstances to accept, and in some instances take a somewhat fatalistic view of, the physical environment which you inherit in a particular school or classroom. None the less, the degree to which features of this working environment assist or hinder your implementation of educational practice on a day-to-day basis depends on the fit between the design and your intended practice. In this chapter we consider the following key points.

(1) The physical setting directly influences the ways people behave, and so should be taken into account when managing the children's behaviour in classroom settings.

(2) The ways people use space, where and how they sit or stand in relation to other people, form part of their *communication* with others.

(3) Different seating arrangements are therefore suited to, and preferred for, activities and interactions of different kinds.

(4) It follows that different room and seating arrangements should be chosen in class according to the activities which are planned. The setting will then encourage children to behave in ways which are appropriate to their tasks.

The physical setting provided by your classroom will influence pupils' behaviour, both directly and via its effects on other people's behaviour — including your own (Glynn, 1982; Wheldall, 1981). Certain features of your classroom will be beyond your direct control. However there are others which you can and must arrange so that you and your classroom 'speak with one voice' as to how children should behave. Organise your classroom and its contents well, and they will work with you to encourage 'good' behaviour.

TAKING ACCOUNT OF YOUR CLASSROOM

There are a number of factors which together make up the physical component of the classroom environment. We consider them briefly in turn, as you will need to take account of each in managing your classroom so that it works with you.

Visual factors

There are two aspects which need to be considered. The first, of course, is the quality of illumination in different parts of the room, which will be determined by the level of natural and artificial light available. The second concerns the way the classroom environment is arranged. Is it visually stimulating? Does it create the atmosphere you want? Do displays excite and capture the children's interest? Are there any unwanted distractions, such as windows overlooking the playing field? What will the children learn about *you* from the way the visual environment is arranged?

Acoustic factors

With such heavy reliance on verbal communication and the need to avoid distractions, acoustic factors are of considerable importance in the classroom. In the United Kingdom, guidelines concerning visual and acoustic factors have been offered by the Department of Education and Science (Department of Education and Science, 1981a and 1981b).

Noise in particular is something to which most teachers are sensitive. Its effects on performance and behaviour have been investigated in a wide range of studies (see Porteous, 1977). Clearly the extent to which a classroom is affected by noise depends not only on the school's design but also on its organisation and the teaching methods employed. What are the main sources of unnecessary noise in your room: the corridor outside, scraping chairs, the children — yourself? What steps can you take to damp down classroom noise? How does the timetable affect the noise suffered by — and produced by — your class? What levels of conversation and other sounds would you judge to be reasonable during activities of different kinds? Which activities can be run in parallel and which would be incompatible due to noise distractions? No less than visual factors, the acoustic environment will contribute to classroom atmosphere: from the concentrated silence of a library to the clamour of the market place!

Thermal factors

The heating and ventilation requirements of British schools are again subject to regulations and guidelines (for example, Department of Education and Science, 1972 and 1981b). Climatic variables are most definitely beyond a teacher's control and the control of the heating system may seem equally so! None the less thermal conditions play an important part in making the environment seem comfortable or otherwise. Moreover there is sufficient evidence

47

from studies to suggest that they can and do influence performance and behaviour (Bell, Fisher and Loomis, 1978).

Spatial factors

The spatial design of schools and their teaching areas have altered considerably over the years. Changes reflect not only economic and social factors, but also trends in educational practice (Manning, 1967). A number of publications are available in the United Kingdom which outline desirable features for inclusion in the design of educational settings, and the adaptation and remodelling of school buildings (see, for example, Institute of Advanced Architectural Studies, 1976; Department of Education and Science, 1984).

The effects of spatial design on the behaviour of the occupants in a variety of settings, including classrooms, have been explored by Sommer (1969, 1974). He emphasises that the design of school buildings and their influences should be of concern to teachers as well as architects since teachers have to manage the classroom environment. As Manning (1967) suggests, the skills of good teachers 'are likely to be stretched to the greatest advantage in buildings that are designed to provide the greatest amount of flexibility — in other words, in buildings which effect the least hindrance to anything the teachers may wish to do' (p. 62).

In keeping with the rest of our book, we shall not dwell further on those factors which are unlikely to come within a teacher's direct influence. Rather we shall concentrate on one aspect of the physical environment over which the teacher does have direct control: the organisation of classroom space and the people within it.

SHARING SPACE WITH OTHER PEOPLE

We start by considering how people behave in relation to their physical environment and apply this information to the organisation of classroom space.

With few exceptions at home, at work and in public places, we share spaces with other people. In our patterns of movement, our choice of seating and our interactions with others we exhibit *spatial behaviours*. These have the obvious functions of preventing us falling over one another and maintaining enough space for each of us to work in. However, studies have also confirmed the importance of spatial behaviours in our communication with other people and in securing different degrees of privacy.

Findings from research in this area can be usefully applied to the classroom setting. They confirm the simple and obvious point that, by arranging the furniture in particular ways, we can set the scene for interactions between children, and between child and teacher, which are appropriate to learning on particular types of activity.

It would be a relatively easy task to set out simply a series of classroom arrangements which, on the basis of research, would seem suited to different types of activity. However, as we have already pointed out, recipes alone are difficult to adapt and to apply to a range of different situations. The consistent use of room arrangement as an integral part of management in the classroom requires that a teacher can make informed choices and adapt arrangements to suit particular circumstances. Freedom to do so involves, in our view, a working knowledge of spatial behaviours and their relationship to patterns of social interaction. We shall therefore begin by illustrating what we mean by 'spatial behaviours', with the help of some everyday examples.

What are spatial behaviours?

These are patterns of behaviour through which each of us maintains a private space around us and in which we tolerate or invite the presence of other people only under particular circumstances. Usually only a very small circle of 'significant' others are afforded this privilege: our partner or spouse, close family and friends. Acquaintances may be invited within our personal space under particular circumstances. The presence of Christmas mistletoe is, for many, one such predisposing factor! We accept the close proximity of total strangers only under very specific circumstances such as when we attend a medical or dental examination or find ourselves in overcrowded places. Otherwise strangers are, by definition, unwelcome.

Our personal space centres on our body and surrounds each of us whatever we are doing. Its boundaries are invisible and may vary. Usually we are made aware of our own so-called 'bubble' of privacy only when someone has intruded without invitation. Consider how you would react in the following situations: you are sitting on an empty bus and a stranger gets on and sits next to you; you are queuing and the person behind you accidentally brushes against you — for the third time; you are walking and talking with a friend in the street and you find an oncomer heading directly for the small space between you; the salesman keeps emphasising his point by laying his hand on your arm. Each of these represents an unauthorised invasion of personal space.

When such intrusions occur we may feel uncomfortable or ill at ease. We are also likely to take some form of compensatory action, perhaps by moving away or changing body position, by erecting a barrier such as a newspaper or shopping bag or by avoiding eye contact with the intruder. Invasions of personal space may not only have effects on the victim but also on the invader. We go to some lengths to avoid even approaching others' personal space. You may have noticed this yourself when, for example, altering your course to avoid individuals and groups on the pavement.

Faced with situations in which personal space invasions are inevitable we seek to reduce their effects on ourselves and others. We may give initial signals to prepare the victim for our imminent invasion, perhaps by seeking their permission with 'Excuse me', 'May I?' or by offering apologies. If we must squeeze past a stranger we orientate ourselves carefully, minimising contact and avoiding their eyes, so reducing the potential embarrassment for both parties. Overcrowding presents an extreme set of circumstances. The traveller in the crowded tube train or lift may be unable to move and must tolerate strangers pressing on all sides. These situations are coped with by treating others as if they were 'part of the background' or non-persons. The traveller stands rigid and gazes fixedly at the wall, floor or at some distant point, strictly avoiding eye contact and communication.

Now consider situations when you are choosing a seat in a public place, for example in the park. Compare where you would sit when the park bench is empty with your choice if there is already one occupant. Where would you sit if the person were at one end of the bench? If they were seated in the centre what would you do? Where you sit and how you sit are examples of spatial behaviour. Again people choose different seating distances and positions according to whom they are with and what they are doing.

The common observations that many visiting speakers must address their audience across an empty row or two, and that lecture theatres often fill up from the back reflect the spatial behaviour of individual audience members. Their choice of seat will be largely determined by their readiness to become involved during the session. Imagine the consternation if a speaker began by moving to the back of the room and asked his audience to turn their chairs around!

Studies of spatial behaviour

We shall consider here three groups of studies whose findings seem to us to have implications for your organisation of classroom space. First we summarise findings from studies of personal space requirements among adults and children. We then consider the spatial behaviours people show during interactions with others. Finally, we explore observations on the seating arrangements people choose for different types of activity.

Personal space behaviour

An intriguing selection of studies reported by Porteous (1977) and Bell, Fisher and Loomis (1978) combine to indicate that personal space requirements vary according to culture, sex and certain personal characteristics. People of higher status are accorded more space, and personal space also operates at the group level. However, an individual's requirements would seem to be remarkably consistent.

Interpersonal distance and communication

The distance at which two people position themselves in face-to-face contact reflects, in part, the personal space requirements of each when interacting with the other. However, the situation is more complex than this, for the distance people choose does not depend solely upon whether or not they are strangers. It depends upon more subtle differences in the acquaintance between them and also upon where they are and what they are doing. The reason for this is that interpersonal distance is part of their interaction. It is one form of *communication*.

The total message that we give to those with whom we interact involves not only the spoken word but also non-verbal signals. These are given by our voice tone, eye contact, facial expression, our gestures and body position, by touch and sometimes even by smell. The distance at which two people place themselves is therefore important, for it determines the senses which will be most involved in the verbal and non-verbal communications between them. It follows that each person will choose a distance which provides him

51

with comfortable levels of verbal and non-verbal information from the other. Therefore, if one person positions himself incorrectly this can lead to miscommunication or misinterpretation. They might be quite literally too 'distant' or 'too close for comfort'! The other party may then need to compensate by changing position so that, for them, a more comfortable distance is restored. Such compensatory actions are also likely to follow if inappropriate use is made of other forms of communication: for example, if one person speaks too loudly, gestures too dramatically or looks too hard and too long.

Adults and children interact at closer ranges with people they like (see, for example, Guardo, 1969; Edwards, 1972) or who are in some way — in culture, status, interests or age — similar to themselves (see, for example, Willis, 1966; Heshka and Nelson, 1972; Scherer, 1974). Both adults and children give most attention to an interaction when they are placed at comfortable distances from one another, that is, at distances which may be seen to meet *personal* space requirements (Albert and Dabbs, 1970; Krantz and Risley, 1977).

As we may predict from findings on personal space, there are differences in interpersonal distancing with cultural, sex, age and personal variables. However, the rules are strict, so that a third party can interpret the distancing between two people and estimate the nature of their acquaintance and the interaction (Hall, 1966; Russo, 1967).

Seating position and types of activity

On the basis of our everyday experience and the research findings considered so far, we could predict that people will choose different seating positions for privacy and for interactions of various types. A series of studies reported by Sommer (1969) explored the choices of seating made by students and by children for activities which involve differing kinds of interaction.

Individual working. As we might anticipate, when people wish to work privately and without interruption from others, they choose seats which are well apart from other people. Seats which prevent or reduce eye contact either by their positioning or by screening are preferred by students and children. People will attempt to *avoid* others, choosing a seat at the end of a table or near the wall. Alternatively they try to *defend* privacy by keeping others away, choosing chairs which dominate a table from the aisle or centre.

Cooperative working. People will sit close together so they can talk and share materials when working together. The preferred seating arrangement for both children and students is to sit side by side with the friend with whom they are working cooperatively.

Competitive working. When working competitively people will choose to sit further apart yet in a position which enables them to check on how well the other is doing. The preferred position for students is to be opposite a partner with whom they are competing as this increases eye contact and stimulates competition. Children's choices would seem to be affected by the width of the table.

The findings for individual, cooperative and competitive working are summarised in Figure 4.1.

Figure 4.1: Preferred seating arrangements for pairs working on different kinds of activity. X = preferred seating positions

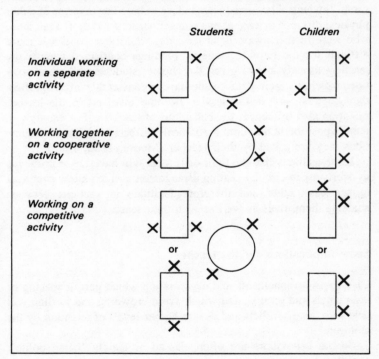

Source: adapted from Sommer, 1969.

53

Participation in larger groups

A number of studies (Sommer, 1969, 1974; Sommer and Olsen, 1980) have investigated the relationship between student participation, group size and seating location in lectures and seminar situations. From your own experience you may expect that the larger the group, the less participation by students, and this is borne out by findings.

Participation was also found to relate to seating arrangement when comparisons were made across groups of similar size (twenty or so). Straight-row seating plans were least favourable, more contributions being offered by students when seats were arranged in a horseshoe or open square layout. Circular arrangements would seem to be most conducive to student participation and, as we may predict, the highest rate of contribution by students was found when circular seating was combined with comfortable 'soft' surroundings!

Furthermore, participation varied with students' location in the room. Students who were located close to the tutor in terms of either physical distance or ease of eye contact participated more than those who were further away, or at the sides where eye contact is more difficult for the tutor to achieve. Findings confirmed what many teachers already know: given the choice, students will sit in positions which, by their distance and the eye contact they afford, reflect their interest and willingness to become involved in the lesson. Location also influences the behaviour of teachers. For example, a pupil's position in the room dramatically affects the number of questions they are asked by their teacher (Moore, 1980, 1982).

It seems likely that the tutor or teacher will have fewer problems to overcome in circular seating arrangements which allow everyone to see each other and therefore facilitate interactions between students themselves as well as with their teacher.

Some implications for the teacher

Classroom arrangements and organisation which permit spacing of individuals and groups, and which avoid crowding and jostling will help to reduce conflicts and ensure higher levels of attention by the children.

Spatial behaviours are often classed as simply 'being polite': avoiding pushing past others, saying 'Excuse me' and not invading adults' personal space in the corridor or at the teacher's desk. It is important to recognise that children may not interpret these invasions in the same way as adults do, and may be surprised and puzzled by strong negative reactions. Nevertheless, the busy school environment provides ideal opportunities for learning this group of skills. The adult staff can play an important role in teaching children appropriate spatial behaviours and their social implications.

We have seen that adults and children prefer different seating positions, according to the type of interaction entailed in activities of different kinds. It follows that if we wish children to interact in ways best suited to a particular type of classroom activity, then we should encourage appropriate behaviour by placing the seating in ways closely resembling the preferred positions. Conversely, we should avoid seating arrangements which are likely to encourage unwanted patterns of interaction among the children, or which discourage their participation when it is needed.

We go on to consider in closer detail the choice of seating arrangements for classroom activities of different kinds.

SPEAKING WITH ONE VOICE: YOUR CHOICE OF ROOM ARRANGEMENT

The arrangement and organisation of the room itself is an integral and fundamental part of classroom management. In preparing the room the teacher is literally setting the scene for the events that will take place during a teaching session. How can you successfully incorporate the arrangement of your classroom in your lesson plans so that the room works *with* you, assisting your management of the children's behaviour during the lesson?

Obviously, your choice of layout will be determined by the learning activities which you intend the children to undertake. Different activities will have their own implications for the following aspects of room arrangement.

Aspects of room arrangement

Children's interactions with each other

What kinds of interaction are best suited to the activity? Which seating arrangement would be most favourable for this pattern of interaction?

Children's use of materials

Do the children require individual sets of materials or will they share? Where should materials be located? Can everyone see the relevant visual displays?

Children's interactions with the teacher

What role do you, the teacher, have during the activity? Will you be the main source of help and direction, or will you direct children to each other for help or ideas? How can you make sure that everyone can see and hear you when necessary?

Patterns of movement

All the above factors have implications for patterns of movement around the room. How much movement by the children should be involved? How can you ensure easy access to materials? Which arrangement enables you to reach the children easily or vice versa?

Let us consider activities of different types in turn, exploring their implications for these aspects of classroom management and organisation.

Working alone

Individual working is preferable for activities which involve the learning of new skills or factual information where each child needs to be able to work without distractions and interruptions by others. Many tasks in basic skill areas are of this type, for example, number and comprehension exercises and worksheets of various kinds. Children should be seated well apart, and distractions by other people can be minimised by providing each child with his own set of materials, together with complete instructions about the task.

During this type of activity the teacher is the primary source of information, help and encouragment, providing the necessary instructions to begin with and assisting during the activity. She therefore needs easy access to all the children and a seating plan which allows her to monitor what everyone is doing so that she can respond quickly when help is needed. Note that we describe the teacher going to the children rather than the other way round, so limiting the distraction of movement by others, and the possibility that her vision becomes obscured by children waiting their turn at her desk.

Working cooperatively

On cooperative activities children work together, in pairs or small groups, to achieve a joint goal. They share materials and help each other: to complete a written task; to solve a mathematics problem; to undertake a joint project; or to carry out a science experiment. Each group's task may be quite unrelated to those on which other groups are working. Alternatively, children may be working on their group's contribution to a whole class production, such as a frieze or class newspaper. Cooperative groupwork is also a useful way to increase the opportunities for all to participate in discussions. Having talked about a topic separately within small groups each group could then put forward a summary of its ideas, views or conclusions to a whole class 'plenary' session.

By definition, this type of activity involves the children in high levels of interaction with others in their group. They are expected not only to share materials but to offer ideas, information and help in contributing to the group's completion of a task. Johnson and Johnson (1975) propose mixed group composition so that individual members bring different skills and can help one another where skills are weak.

Groups of varying size could be seated in clusters of chairs or around tables so that all members of a group can see each other and talk without shouting. Of course, the amount of space allocated to each group will depend upon the activity and the levels of movement it involves. Since each group works independently of others, separation, by distancing and perhaps also by screening, will be necessary. The degree of movement needed beyond a group's working space will largely depend upon the location of resources. These may be distributed among groups, or children may require access to centrally located materials, to the sink, etc.

When children are working together they use their teacher less for help and support. The teacher's involvement is directed towards introducing and maintaining the activity, clarifying the task and stimulating discussion. He refers pupils to each other for information and help, rather than providing suggestions or solutions himself. He will also wish to address the whole class from time to time and obviously some changes in seating arrangements might then be needed.

Working competitively

Here we refer to children competing with each other, rather than with their own previous performance on a task. The latter would be more likely to involve individual working.

In competitive activities children are working against each other towards a goal set by the teacher and the winners meet the goal at the losers' expense. Johnson and Johnson (1975) argue that the use of this type of activity should be restricted to skills practice or information recall, where the emphasis is on speed. Competitive activities are, of course, familiar in games and PE lessons, and in the classroom often take the form of quizzes of various kinds. The light-hearted 'game' element should be stressed, the intention being that competitive situations are enjoyable.

The interactions between children who are competing with one another are more limited than on cooperative tasks. Nevertheless, there is some interaction and movement, for each child needs to keep a check on his opponents' progress and actions in order to monitor his own performance. Groups will need to be made up of members having similar skill levels so that each member has a reasonable chance of winning within his group.

Whilst children monitor their own performance in comparison with others on competitive activities, the teacher remains their major source of help, clarification and encouragement. He is also the arbitrator in the event that disputes arise! In addition to moving about between groups he may need access to a visual display or scoreboard. From here he will most probably address the whole group, particularly at the beginning and end of the activity and again some changes in seating may then be needed.

The point of competitive activities is to enliven tasks which involve repeated practice of skills or rehearsal of information. They should be *enjoyable* activities — win or lose.

A comparison of these three types of activity and their implications for classroom organisation is shown in Table 4.1.

Mixed activities: mixed seating patterns

In a variety of learning activities the three basic types of working we have described are likely to occur in combination. For example, members of a group who are working together on a joint project may well share out different parts of the task and work individually on these for a time. Perhaps each will be reading about one aspect of the topic, or working on separate elements of a frieze, after mapping it out together. In these cases a room arrangement which incorporates both separate and group work spaces would be indicated.

During other activities members of a group may work together, but in competition with other groups. The room's layout should allow members to work closely together, free from eavesdropping by other teams, and yet allow them to keep an eye on the progress of their opponents.

On some individual tasks a teacher may encourage children to help one another to some extent, perhaps with spellings during a storywriting activity. However, he would wish the content of the stories to be each child's own. Therefore, whilst he may allow some proximity to classmates, any conversations would be expected to be brief and he would not want children to be able to read others' stories. He might therefore choose fairly well spaced groupings around tables. Similar arrangements may be used when children work on their own creations during craftwork but require access to shared materials or equipment.

Since many variations are possible and a sequence of different activities may imply several changes in layout, a teacher could be forgiven for being overwhelmed at the prospect! A more settled room arrangement is, of course, achieved by using what we would term a 'mixed economy' layout, different areas of the room being designated for certain types of activity. Separate seating may be provided in one section, whilst in others seats could be grouped in various ways. Some differentiation of classroom space is familiar in many nursery and primary schools. Quite distinct 'interest areas' are often provided for craftwork, library, water play and so on. This pattern is further extended in open-plan nursery and primary settings. They often have clear divisions between areas which are equipped for different activities, and these may also differ in size, floor coverings, furniture and storage facilities. When arranging these different spaces within your classroom, essential considerations will be: their screening; the choice of seating patterns best suited to the activities which are to take place; the location of materials; and the allowance of space for movement.

The advantages of a 'mixed economy' layout are that the children, rather than the furniture, are allocated to different places as activities change and that activities can run in parallel during an 'integrated' session. Thus, this type of organisation permits both flexibility and a settled room arrangement.

Table 4.1: Comparison of activity types

Activity type	Type of task	Grouping	Access to each other	Access to materials	Access to teacher	Patterns of movement	Seating arrangement
Individual	Acquisition of new skills or factual information (for example, learning new number skills, reading for comprehension)	Children work alone	Children work separately on their own task, contact with others is minimised	Each child has complete set of materials and is given full instructions on how to use them	Frequent contact with the teacher who is each child's main source of help, feedback and encouragement	Children's movement is minimal; teacher needs clear access to each individual	Each child is separated as far as possible spatially and by seating position, (using separate desks or row arrangements if possible)
Competitive	Simple skills practice, or rehearsal of information, with emphasis on speed and quantity of work (for example, quizzes or 'games'	Children are grouped so as to provide equal chances of winning	Children monitor each other's progress; they work in clusters with some talking and movement	Individual sets or complete set of materials for each cluster; children need instructions on how to use materials and follow the rules, for example, taking turns	Less use of teacher feedback, which is obtained by comparison with others; teacher is main source of help and encouragement, and also arbitrates!	Some movement by children; teacher needs clear access to clusters and displays	Children are clustered in small groups; sitting so they have good eye contact and keep track of their opponents' progress; clusters well separated, so members can move further apart from each other if needed during the contest

| Cooperative | Problem-solving or creative activities, (for example, topic work; craft-work; science experiment; discussion; or simulation exercise) | Children may be grouped in a variety of ways, which bring together different skills | Children interact with each other as the main source of help, information and feedback. They work in clusters. Movement varies with task | A set of materials for each group and/or centrally located materials; children need information on what is available | Each child makes less use of the teacher for help feedback and encouragement; teacher directs them to their group for these but clarifies the task, stimulates discussion and encourages the group | Freedom of movement by the children, clear access lanes between groups and to central materials | Children are clustered in small groups of chairs or around tables, so that each can see all others in the group and talk without shouting |

Source: adapted from Johnson and Johnson, 1975.

Even if you choose a 'mixed economy' layout as your basic room arrangement there will still be occasions when you will need to change parts of the room, or all of it, to suit certain activities. You may even wish the whole class to be seated in traditional 'rows' for an activity which involves all class members in responding at the same time, or perhaps for a formal 'presentation' by one group to an audience of classmates.

One final point

Studies have indicated that the physical setting not only influences behaviour (Glynn, 1982) but that it also conveys information about the *people* associated with that setting. That is, features of a room, such as its layout or tidiness can lead to inferences about the people who work there. For example, Weinstein and Woolfolk (1981) found that adults' ratings of the unknown teachers and pupils associated with different empty classrooms were affected by the layout of the room. 'Open' classrooms with 'interest areas' led to more positive ratings by adults than did 'traditional' classrooms. Interestingly room arrangement did not affect the judgements made by ten-year-old children taking part in this study.

Whatever the classroom's arrangement, however, adults and children alike judged teachers associated with tidy rooms more favourably than those in messy rooms. Neatness affected judgements not only about teachers' organisation, but also about their kindliness and inventiveness. Moreover, pupils associated with neat rooms were rated as happier and better behaved than those in untidy rooms. There is a need for confirmation from research inside classrooms and with teacher and pupils present. However, these findings underline the need to take care of your classroom and make sure it creates the impression you would want!

SUMMARY

In Chapter 4 we have considered the setting for children's behaviour provided by the classroom and its organisation. We outlined several factors which need to be taken into account when managing the physical environment: visual, auditory, thermal and spatial factors. We then focused on the organisation of classroom space.

We discussed research findings on spatial behaviours, their relationship to communication and implications for the teacher. We introduced three basic seating arrangements which are suited to, and preferred for, activities and interactions of different types. Each of these seating arrangements can be used to encourage children's appropriate behaviour during learning activities of different kinds depending on whether children are to work individually, cooperatively or competitively.

We then discussed a teacher's choice of room arrangement according to the activities planned and their implications for patterns of interaction and movement, seating and materials. The chapter concluded with observations as to what a classroom's layout and tidiness may say about the teacher and pupils who work there.

Your room may well have limitations in its size or shape, or the storage units and furniture you have to work with. You may have to make compromises, not least because you have only a limited number of certain materials. Whatever its limitations, the classroom environment *is* yours to use as part of your approach to management. Organised well, your 'talking' classroom will work for you. It will help you to encourage those behaviours from the children which are compatible with their tasks and discourage those which are inappropriate. The management of behaviour from the beginning, through your organisation of the classroom setting and the events within it will help to free you to praise, rather than correct, the children's behaviour. Thus it will also set the scene for a *positive system of management*.

5

Leading Them into 'Good' Habits

INTRODUCTION

In this chapter we are concerned with what happens once the room
is occupied, when teacher and pupils come together to form a working group. How does the teacher manage this *social* context in which
children's behaviour takes place?

Like any organised group, the class group has a leader, in this
case of course, their teacher. We therefore consider first a teacher's
role in her capacity as leader, in particular examining the importance
of her behaviour and responsibilities in this role. Next we consider
teacher expectations about children's behaviour. How can you be
sure that pupils are really clear about what you expect of them?
Finally we outline some of the procedures which teachers use to help
children behave in appropriate ways. Our emphasis is upon using
these procedures and your own behaviour most *effectively* in the
group situation.

YOUR ROLE AS LEADER

We have outlined (Chapter 4) how a teacher can begin to manage
interactions, movement and allocation of space and materials by
careful room management. Once pupils enter the room the teacher
exercises control over events by group management in the role of
leader.

The role of leader is an essential complement to that of teacher.
As leader the teacher ensures that each teaching session can progress
smoothly and efficiently, without confusion or the need for *ad hoc*
decisions as to how to proceed. In this role the teacher ensures that

the entire class group, subgroups and individuals within it can operate effectively. For this to happen it is necessary to manage communication and the use of space and materials within the room. Obviously lessons would be impossible were all present to speak at once, or could move about and use materials as the fancy took them!

Many experienced teachers and teacher-trainers stress the importance of establishing one's position as leader very early in the initial contacts with a new group. Effective leadership is particularly important during these early sessions. It is then that you need to establish, and rapidly teach, those pupil behaviours which are appropriate in the group context, so that educational proceedings can run smoothly from the outset. Your credibility as leader will depend on how you take up the rights and responsibilities which are associated with the position.

Behaving as a leader

Effective leadership is dependent on the acceptance or acknowledgement of the leader's authority by all group members. Without this acceptance individual members of the group, or factions within it, are likely to question the leadership of the incumbent in a variety of ways. These would, at the least, interrupt lessons and might escalate into major confrontations between challenger and teacher. Many student and probationary teachers are all too aware of this. Unfortunately their efforts to establish authority may sometimes lead them to behave in ways which are paradoxically counterproductive. Let us illustrate this with two examples of first meetings.

Mrs Smith determines to make up for her lack of height by strength of will and personality when she meets her first fourth year class. She will show them who's boss from the start! Therefore whenever she enters class she marches into the room and positions herself close to the children at the front tables. She calls the class group to pay attention in her most commanding tones and sharply reprimands those who continue to talk. Then she stands glaring around the faces before her, ready to act swiftly if anyone 'steps out of line'.

Whilst Mrs Smith hopes to dominate the group, her behaviour expresses an assumption that her authority is under threat and that she needs to defend it. Her pupils may soon begin to test out her

65

authority not, as she fears, because of her small size but because her behaviour conveys *insecurity* rather than her security in the leadership role.

Mr Jones is a gentle giant and is aware that young children may be apprehensive when faced with their first male teacher. He therefore decides to win the approval and respect of his first year juniors by being friendly and showing interest in the children as individuals. When he enters the classroom he moves quietly to his seat and sits down so that his height will be less awesome from the children's viewpoint. He returns the smiles of children who notice his presence and responds pleasantly to their questions until the rest of the class begin to settle down. Then he asks, 'Is everybody ready?'.

Mr Jones is at pains to appear friendly and to minimise the possibility that his size and sex may work against him. However, in doing so, his behaviour conveys a willingness to *follow* his pupils rather than to *lead* them. His self-effacing manner and failure to take the initiative in early sessions could result in his young charges running rings around him!

The problem is that in neither example does the teacher behave in ways which are consistent with leadership. The paradox is that, in order to convey his/her position as leader in the group, a teacher must behave as if leadership is already established! That is, the teacher must demonstrate his/her leadership, and must behave in ways consistent with the *higher status* attendant upon his/her position as leader (Robertson, 1981).

Studies have shown that certain rights are associated with higher status. For example, people with higher status are afforded more spatial mobility. So, as leader, a teacher is permitted to move easily and freely about all parts of the classroom and should do so. As 'followers' of their leader the pupils, on the other hand, must first be given this right by their teacher.

We have already noted (see Chapter 4) the important contribution which body posture, expression, eye contact and gesture make to communication. It may not be surprising therefore, that these non-verbal aspects of communication play important roles in conveying status. If, when talking to pupils, a teacher's manner is too aggressive or too submissive, if he avoids his pupils' eyes, or if he nervously fiddles with his collar, he is unlikely to convey leadership. Higher status is conveyed by a relaxed posture, a pleasant matter-of-fact tone and manner and by engaging, rather than avoiding, eye contact with pupils. Note that erect and attentive body posture together with a return of eye contact is usually expected from pupils in conversation with their teachers. To behave in these ways is to acknowledge the teacher's relative status.

Usually people with higher status are expected to take the lead during interactions. The teacher as leader should therefore be the initiator in conversations with pupils through seeking eye contact and speaking first. He also keeps the initiative and is the person who closes the interaction. A pupil who takes the initiative and puts the leader in the answering role, or a pupil who frequently 'must have the last word' are not behaving in accordance with their role as followers. Both may meet with disapproval from their teacher!

Higher status also permits the teacher to interrupt pupils' activities or conversations with one another. The teacher uses this right when she stops the group to give an explanation or instructions. She must also use it in order to manage communication between members of the group and to safeguard the rights of individuals to speak and be heard. Conversely children may not interrupt their teacher!

We have already noted that people with higher status are afforded greater personal space by others. Furthermore, whilst intrusions by very young children into an adult's space are acceptable, less tolerance is given to older children. As both adult and leader then, the teacher can expect pupils to afford her greater space and with the exception of very young children, pupils are not expected to lean on her desk, or to push past her. However, her position does afford her the right to enter the personal space of pupils and even to pick up the materials they are using.

These then are some of the small but telling actions which convey a teacher's position as leader. Demonstrating leadership in these ways can assist your credibility during the crucial early sessions with a new group. However, taking up status rights is not the whole story. The leadership role carries responsibilties as well as rights.

Responsibilities as a leader

The first responsibility is to avoid the overuse of leadership rights. Pupils convey their acceptance of a teacher's leadership to the extent that their behaviour is consistent with their role as followers and they permit the teacher's higher status behaviour without challenge. A teacher can only lead with their consent.

Other group members too have their rights, and the second responsibility of the leader is to safeguard these. Pupils have the right to sufficient space and materials, to speak and to be heard. They have the right to be treated *fairly* and with courtesy and respect.

Certain responsibilities to the group begin well before the first session. These involve careful preparation, planning and organisation of the classroom and the activities which are to take place. Even if there has not been an opportunity to meet the children, a teacher can begin this process by becoming familiar with the class through completed school records. Records which contain details of the skills children have been taught, difficulties experienced, and any special requirements which individuals have, will help inform the choice of early activities. Similarly, balanced information about the children's social behaviour can contribute to decisions about reasonable and fair expectations for future behaviour. At the simplest level, knowing all the children's names and being able to put names to faces allows a teacher direct communication with children from the start and helps convey interest in them as individuals.

Finally, a teacher has the responsibility to be punctual: to be there when the class arrives and to start and finish lessons on time.

In the longer term a teacher's credibility as leader rests on behaviour in the role of *teacher* as well as actions as a leader. If children's work is carefully chosen and prepared, if lessons are interesting and children can see they are being helped to learn, a teacher's credibility as both teacher and leader is likely to be firmly established.

Making expectations clear to the children

We have explored the importance of *non-verbal* communication in defining the relationships between teacher and pupils. Of course the ways in which teacher and children use *language* in the classroom is a further powerful expression of their relationship with each other. Stubbs (1976) suggests that 'by the very way in which a teacher talks to his pupils, he inevitably communicates to them his definition of the situation and the form of relationship which he considers appropriate' (pp. 167–8). His study, in a secondary school context, highlighted the subtle ways in which classroom language is used to define teacher and pupil roles and to keep them in touch with one another.

When they make references to the shared experiences and personal knowledge which members of a group develop in the longer term, teacher and pupils reinforce social relationships within the group and humorous references of this kind sometimes provide a means of social control by the teacher (Walker and Adelman, 1976). That jokes and humour can also be used by pupils to challenge their teacher's authority is illustrated by Torode (1976).

Here we shall concentrate upon the teacher's use of language to communicate her expectations of children's behaviour in class.

Sources of teacher expectations

Teacher expectations will vary according to a number of factors. First there are those relating to the teacher herself: her training, her professional and personal experience and her awareness of ethical issues. Secondly there are considerations based on her information about the children: their ages, educational and social skills and their previous learning experiences at school and home. Then there are factors relating to the classroom setting and the educational and social events which are to take place.

Finally, and based on all of these, will be the variety of social behaviours which the teacher wishes pupils to learn and maintain. These will be behaviours which assist the smooth running of the teaching environment. They will include a range of behaviours relating to the ways children interact with each other, with their teacher and their tasks, their movement around the room and their use of materials and equipment. Social behaviours will also encompass the children's responses to their teacher's management of communication, movement and so on.

The teacher brings these different factors together in a set of clear and reasonable expectations of children's behaviour. Expectations will need to be tailored to a particular group of children working within a certain classroom environment. They will also need to fit within the broader expectations which pertain in the wider school environment.

Clarifying expectations

The behavioural framework enables teachers to define expectations in terms of the observable behaviours which would be considered appropriate or inappropriate to a particular context. Some behaviours such as stopping and looking at the teacher when instructed to do so may always be desired, whereas others will be appropriate in some, but not all, situations. There are certain actions, such as swearing, which are unacceptable whatever the circumstances.

Communicating expectations to pupils

If a teacher relied solely on his general organisation of classroom events to convey his expectations as to how pupils should behave, children could become confused as to what is required of them. It is important to make expectations *explicit* to pupils by actually describing them. Throughout the day a teacher makes different kinds of statements to pupils: about classroom rules and routines, activities children are working on and how they should work together. How can a teacher most clearly express his expectations in the statements he makes?

The first consideration is a willingness to state the obvious. Thus a teacher might assume that the class will listen when he is talking or stay in their places when working. However, not all children may share his view of things, so even such basic expectations may need to be explained initially.

Secondly, it is essential to choose words the pupils will be certain to understand. As a general rule words which describe observable events and behaviours (such as, 'take turns', 'when the bell goes', 'sit and wait quietly', 'hand in your English books') are more easily understood than less specific descriptions (such as, 'be polite', 'concentrate', 'put your things over there'). Findings during a small local survey (Solity, in preparation) involving teachers of 7 to 8-year-olds suggested that there is a tendency to be more explicit in telling pupils what is *not wanted* than in stating what is *wanted*. For example, 'don't shout out' is more specific than 'settle down'.

In a *positive* management system it is essential to communicate to children what they *can or should do* rather than spell out what they should not do. Telling pupils what not to do risks leaving them in doubt as to what *is* required. Negative phrasing also risks putting ideas into children's heads, increasing the likelihood that the misbehaviour referred to will occur!

When your statements focus on appropriate behaviour and are worded in specific terms relating to observable events, children will be helped greatly in meeting your expectations.

SIGNPOSTS TO 'GOOD' BEHAVIOUR

These are procedures which teachers use specifically to draw pupils' attention to the behaviour required in particular circumstances or to underline those classroom behaviours which are almost always required. *Rules, routines, demonstrations* and *directions* are more obvious examples but we also include *modelling* through the behaviour of teacher and children and the use of *visual cues*.

Once established as effective setting events for desired behaviours, these procedures play a crucial part in the smooth running of the group's activities. They also reduce the proportion of valuable contact time which is needed for everyday organisation. Therefore, when working with very young children who are not used to group situations, emphasis is on teaching the children how to respond to cues of this kind. Similarly when children change classes they must be helped to adapt to a new teacher's ways of doing things.

We are interested here in how a teacher makes the most of these procedures so that they act as effective cues for desired behaviour. The assumption is made that expectations for pupil behaviour have already been worked out and are ethical, reasonable, explicit and positive.

Rules

The basic ground-rules of the classroom may be implicit in many of the cues and statements which a teacher gives. By stating them as rules, the teacher makes them explicit in a shortened form for the children. Rules are therefore an effective way to cue the most important classroom behaviours which apply over a period of time. In addition to these general classroom rules a teacher could use rules to encourage appropriate behaviour during specific activities. Rules are especially important for activities which are new, complex or potentially hazardous, or which have been associated with problem behaviour in the past.

To be effective, rules must be reasonable and make demands which are appropriate to children's ages and skills. Furthermore, a rule must be consistent with the cues provided by other setting events within the room. To take an obvious example, a rule that children must stay in their seats when working would be unreasonable if they needed access to materials elsewhere in the room!

Rules must also be relevant and *be seen* to be relevant. A

combination of factors including educational, moral, safety and legal considerations, may be taken into account when deciding relevance. However, classroom rules will focus on the way in which tasks are completed and the ways in which interactions, movement and access to materials are to take place within the room. Thus they will usually include:

(1) *rules referring to interactions* between children and with the teacher: such as working independently, helping friends, complying with teacher requests etc.
(2) *rules relating to school work*: such as listening to instructions, working hard, completing work set, etc.
(3) *specific rules based on the particular activity*: access to materials, use of equipment, handing in work, etc.

In constructing an effective set of rules for classroom behaviour the following guidelines should be borne in mind (see also Medland and Vitale, 1984). The guidelines are summarised in Table 5.1.

Table 5.1: Guidelines for constructing rules

Effective rules are:
clearly worded
phrased positively
brief and to the point
few in number

Rules should be clearly worded

As we have pointed out, a description of the desired behaviour itself is most specific and easy to follow. It is possible to use more general terms which describe a set of behaviours sharing the same quality, for example, 'be friendly and helpful'. However it would be essential to make sure that the behaviours included here are clarified for the children when the rule is introduced: by describing them and giving positive and negative examples of the rule (see p. 74).

Rules should be phrased positively

They should tell children what to do rather than what they should not do. For example, 'Sit quietly when working', 'Put up your hand to ask or tell', 'When Mr Adams claps his hands, look and listen'. Rules which are expressed positively carry the implication that desirable consequences will follow compliance. Conversely, stressing the 'don'ts' by phrasing rules negatively will only serve to highlight and encourage the very behaviours you do not want and force you to deal with them more often than you would like!

Rules should be brief and to the point

Thus, they will be easily remembered by teacher and children alike.

The number of rules should be small

If not, children will be unlikely to remember them all. Limiting the list of rules to no more than five will ensure that they are easy to remember and are more likely to be followed. Your preliminary list may therefore be too long. From this choose the rules which you consider to be the most important and relevant in the circumstances. Depending on the group and the activity, you may wish your final choice of rules to reflect an emphasis on interactions, approach to school work or specific requirements of the activity. Alternatively you may select a balanced group which reflects all three aspects of desired classroom behaviour. The way we present rules, phrasing them positively and in clear, brief terms, facilitates the process of communication. Thus rules are explicit to both teacher and pupils and everyone can be clear about what is expected.

Introducing rules to the class

Rules can be introduced in various ways and we would advocate using all of them, especially when dealing with a new class or activity. These are summarised in Table 5.2.

Table 5.2: Introducing rules to the class

(1) Present the rules
(2) Clarify the rules, with positive and negative examples
(3) Ask the class for amendments and suggestions
(4) Display the rules in a prominent position
(5) Give regular reminders of the rules
(6) Express your confidence in the children
(7) Stress positive consequences of following the rules
(8) Draw attention to behaviour which is consistent with the rules

Present the rules

Rules are presented to the class, and written up, in words or pictures, for children to see during the discussion which follows.

Clarify the rules by giving positive and negative examples of each

This can be done by describing and asking for examples, in discussion with the class. Or you might even act out different behaviours and ask the children to say whether each would be keeping a particular rule.

Ask for suggestions from the class about amendments or additional rules

Pupils will be more likely to keep rules to which they feel they have contributed. So it is useful to invite children's suggestions, ask the others for comments on these, and incorporate them if appropriate.

Place the list of rules on display

Choose a conspicuous position so that it will serve as a reminder to you and your pupils during lessons.

Regularly remind children of the rules

You might rehearse the rules with the group each day, or even each session to start with, and continue to give reminders at intervals. Reminders must be given at times *other* than when a rule has been broken (Clarizio, 1980). This may seem unfamiliar, the tendency as indicated by a survey (Solity, in preparation) among first-year junior teachers being to remind pupils of a rule when a transgression has occurred. However, the point is to cue appropriate behaviour and so reduce the likelihood of misbehaviours, particularly those arising when children misunderstand or forget the rules.

Express your confidence in the children

When you start a session by reminding the class about rules make sure you express your confidence that they *will* try and keep them and that they *can* do so. You will give further weight to this by referring to any improvements you have noted so far.

Stress the positive consequences which can follow when pupils keep to the rules

For example, they will do better in their work; they will complete work earlier, so leaving time for free activities or other privileges; they will be helping their teacher to help them learn.

Draw attention to behaviour which is consistent with the rules

When you notice that children are following the rules and comment upon this, you are confirming for them that their behaviour matches with the rule and also giving further positive examples to other children. Note that it is a child's *behaviour* that you are making an example of, not the child, so comments of this kind must be distributed fairly around the class. We deal with the whole issue of consequences for good behaviour, and in particular the use of praise, in detail in Chapters 7 and 8.

Modelling

Those with whom children spend a great deal of their time are candidates for modelling since children are likely to imitate their behaviour. There are a number of features which increase the likelihood that a particular person will act as a model whose behaviour a child will copy. These include the person's status, the extent to which they have 'power' in terms of giving and withholding rewards, and the extent to which the child sees the person as similar to himself.

Modelling by the teacher

Teacher behaviour is likely to be imitated by children as a teacher has high status and, from the children's point of view, has great power and influence over events during school time. Therefore, by behaving in certain ways the teacher himself cues these behaviours by the children. By keeping his own desk tidy and writing neatly on the board or in children's books, he increases the likelihood that the children will also keep their belongings tidy and write neatly. By talking rather than shouting and making positive rather than negative comments around the classroom, the teacher provides a model of these behaviours for the children.

Since modelling by the teacher is an effective way of teaching behaviour, it is essential that the teacher's behaviour is consistent with that desired from the children. Unfortunately, the continuous exposure of a teacher's behaviour to scrutiny by children in his class can also result in *unintentional learning*. For example, he may be aware that his class is becoming increasingly noisy, but be unaware that his own shouting of instructions above the noise actually contributes to the children's louder behaviour.

Becker, Engelmann and Thomas (1975) include a graphic report by a teacher who deliberately altered her own pattern of behaviour to create a calmer atmosphere in her class. She slowed her pace of walking and talking, gave clear, succinct directions and reduced her own irrelevant conversation as well as unnecessary lesson content. She reports:

> The results are astounding. My class now works quietly for long periods of time and is able to clean up much more quickly than before. The children are more relaxed and speak more quietly. They can change from one task to another easily. In general, a calm atmosphere prevails . . . This has reduced my fatigue and tension. This is extremely important because as my tension rises, so does the noise level in the room. Now I feel the children are not as anxious about their efforts and feel freer to bring their questions to me. When I do explode occasionally I get instant attention.
>
> (Mary Thomas in Becker, Engelmann and Thomas, 1975, p. 119).

Modelling by children

In certain circumstances the behaviour of classmates will act as a model which others imitate. Thus a child is likely to imitate the behaviour of a classmate when the consequences of the behaviour are pleasant, and when the classmate is one whom the child sees as similar to himself. For example, if Tom sees his friend Kevin receive a smile and praise for following an instruction quickly and Tom likes to be praised, he is also likely to follow instructions quickly. In this way providing pleasant consequences for appropriate behaviour by one child has a *ripple effect*, eliciting similar behaviour from the children around him.

When using modelling by other children to cue appropriate behaviour, it is important to avoid the trap of consistently rewarding only certain children in the class group. Furthermore an important distinction here is that it is a child's *behaviour* at a particular time which the teacher is intending his peers to imitate, rather than the child *himself*, who is being held up as an example. It is the desirable behaviour and not the child which is being singled out by the teacher.

Demonstration

Demonstration is a specific use of modelling, involving the deliberate presentation of a behaviour for children to learn. Its use is most familiar, of course, in the educational context when new skills are being introduced. For example, the teacher may demonstrate to an individual or group how to hold and cut with scissors, how to form a letter correctly or how to work through a maths problem. Alternatively, a teacher might ask a pupil who can already perform the skill to demonstrate for others, for example, in Dance or PE. In all these situations demonstration is followed by opportunities for the children to practise the new behaviour. It is a particularly useful method when the behaviour is more easily shown than explained, when children do not have the language skills to follow a complicated verbal direction, or when teaching a routine which involves a sequence of behaviours.

Giving directions (instructions)

During any one day a teacher gives many directions to a class of children. Directions are setting events which literally tell children what to do and are so much a part of everyday school life that they may not receive the detailed attention which is required to make them effective.

The effectiveness of a direction is determined not only by the words which are used but also by the way they are delivered. The teacher's posture, facial expression, voice tone and use of gesture all contribute to the total message which is given to the children. Furthermore, a direction is not a single event but a series of steps. These are described in Table 5.3. Directions should also be seen as a two-way interchange as the teacher only moves from one step to the next when the children's behaviour indicates they have listened and understood each step in the process. We shall now briefly consider the five steps in turn.

Table 5.3: Steps involved in giving a direction

Step 1 *Plan* what to do and say
Step 2 *Catch* the children's attention
Step 3 *Tell* them what to do
Step 4 *Check* they understand
Step 5 *Start* them on the task

Step 1: plan

It is important to decide what is to be said before attracting the children's attention so the content of the direction is clear and concise. This avoids the pitfalls associated with postscripts and afterthoughts delivered as, 'Oh, and one more thing . . .' just as the children are about to begin the task. The movement of groups or furniture is a potentially chaotic business so each step in the direction needs particularly careful planning. Otherwise half the group might be found departing from the room before the teacher has finished telling them what to do once they are outside! To avoid this embarrassment, directions involving movement must therefore begin with an instruction to wait until told to move. Equally, complicated directions or those involving several different instructions need to be separated into a series of shorter directions, each to be presented and followed in turn.

Step 2: catch the children's attention

It is essential that each and every child to whom a direction is addressed is watching and listening. The teacher therefore needs to choose a prominent position from which she can be seen and heard and give a brief, clear signal to attract attention, perhaps a clap of the hands or the group's name. The teacher than waits until all eyes are on her before continuing. Position–signal–wait are therefore the key elements of teacher behaviour at this point.

Step 3: tell the children what to do

The content of directions should be brief and clear and be couched in terms that are familiar to the children. A direction should tell pupils what to do rather than what not to do since, like a rule, it is intended to cue appropriate behaviour. Phrasing helps distinguish a direction from a request and makes it clear that the children are intended, rather than invited, to follow the instructions given. Phrasing also helps distinguish a direction from a question. For example, compare the following two messages:

'How many of you had school dinner today?' and

'If you have had school dinner today, put up your hand'.

The first format (question) cues the children to reply en masse with, 'Me', 'Afzal did', 'No, I didn't', and so on. The second format (direction) tells the children what to do in order that the teacher may count them.

Step 4: check the children understand

Children's facial expressions and other behaviour give the teacher an initial indication as to whether they understand what they are to do. This can be supported by asking pupils whether they understand and asking individuals to repeat elements of the direction. It is easier to clarify any uncertainties before action begins rather than pick up the pieces later when things have gone wrong.

Step 5: start the children on the task

When all the children are clear about what they have to do they can be given the signal to start the task.

Sometimes, particularly with very young children, it is necessary to teach direction-following before these can be used as effective cues for behaviour in the everyday classroom setting. The teacher may set up activities and games in which instructions are deliberately arbitrary or are to be followed in a particular order. Directions may be accompanied initially by reminders which help the children follow the instructions correctly. Later on these additional reminders would be gradually withdrawn. Once simple instructions are followed successfully, the content and complexity of the directions can be gradually increased.

Routines

Routines bring a sequence of behaviours under the control of an initial direction. Once taught they are a useful way of cueing unvarying procedures which occur at regular intervals across the day and week. Registration, entering and leaving the classroom, distribution of materials, changing groups or rearranging the furniture are all necessary elements in the school day which can be completed under the direction of a routine. Time spent teaching routines with a new class can ensure that administration and servicing of 'business' proceedings does not intrude into teaching time.

Routines can be taught by demonstration, by giving directions or through a combination of both. For example, if the teacher wished to teach a group of children how to use a particular box of work cards independently, she may introduce the children to the activity by demonstrating each behaviour in the sequence in turn. Then she would take them through the sequence, having them imitate her on each step. Finally the teacher would give the initial direction and the group would complete the chain with only reminders from the

79

teacher which are gradually faded out altogether. Alternatively a teacher may give the initial direction and then give directions for each step separately, waiting for the children to complete each one before moving on to the next step. Following opportunities to practise the routine, these separate directions would be gradually removed. These and other 'follow-my-leader' exercises serve the purpose of teaching each behaviour in the sequence and linking all the behaviours. Thus completing each one provides the cue for starting the next and all are brought under the control of the initial direction.

Visual cues

Verbal directions and reminders prompt the children to do what is expected during particular routines, at changeover times and so on. Visual cues serve the same purpose and are particularly useful in organising the distribution and collection of materials. Colour-coding is a commonly used visual cue associated with books in the reading scheme, work cards, etc. Folders and sets of materials can of course be colour-coded for each group in the class. Name-tags and place names are also common in nursery and infant class settings. Bright boxes always placed in the same parts of the room serve as useful cues in organising the collection and return of children's work. Written messages on the blackboard outline the tasks to be done and in which order. Written signs indicate where items are kept and remind children of the various essential rules which govern behaviour in the classroom.

Once taught and used systematically, visual cues save confusion and avoid wasting time, for example during children's access to and return of materials, and during changeovers between activities (Becker, Engelmann and Thomas, 1975). They can save precious teaching time that you would otherwise spend giving directions and answering children's queries about where things are and what to do next!

SUMMARY

In Chapter 5 we have highlighted the teacher's role as leader and the ways in which teachers influence children's behaviour through their own behaviour in this role.

It is important to establish leadership authority quickly during the early meetings with a new group. The paradox here is that in order to *gain* authority, a teacher must behave as if her authority is *already* established. Leadership is conveyed not only through a teacher's words but through her actions. How she stands, moves and interacts with pupils should be consistent with leadership status.

Pupils have status rights, too. As their leader, a teacher must safeguard the rights of individuals within the group and meet her reponsibilities to all.

A teacher helps children to meet her expectations when these are reasonable, clearly defined, and are made explicit: by explaining to pupils exactly what they *can do and should do* in class.

Finally, by teaching a new group to follow rules, routines, directions and other cues, a teacher helps pupils to behave in appropriate ways from the start. These procedures also reduce the time spent on everyday organisation throughout the school year!

6

Teaching Matters

INTRODUCTION

You directly influence the ways pupils behave not only in your capacity as leader, but in the role as teacher. We have defined teaching as helping pupils to learn faster and more efficiently than they would on their own (after Vargas, 1977). You need to establish and maintain your role as teacher throughout the weeks and terms of the school year, as it is upon your successful organisation and 'performance' in this role that your credibility with pupils will ultimately rest.

In this chapter we discuss the teaching role as it relates to the management of the educational setting events for children's behaviour in class:

(1) The selection of educational tasks
(2) The pattern of activities
(3) Your behaviour in the teaching role.

THE SELECTION OF EDUCATIONAL TASKS

First we outline some important considerations when selecting educational tasks for a particular class, group or individual. When a teacher sets curricular activities at suitable levels of difficulty, and includes variety in the activities she plans, she helps children to start work, keep on working and enjoy their learning activities.

The level of difficulty

Planning a curriculum which is tailored to the needs of your pupils, and making sure that each child is working on appropriate skills and tasks within it, are fundamental prerequisites for effective teaching. In Chapter 3 we highlighted the contribution a behavioural approach can make to curriculum planning: helping teachers to specify their teaching objectives, to keep accurate records of progress and to communicate effectively with pupils and others. We develop this theme in detail elsewhere, with particular reference to children with special needs (Solity and Bull, 1987).

If a child is presented with a task which is too difficult he is likely to delay starting or soon stop working — and he is then likely to do something else. It may be a quiet activity, such as looking out of the window, or he may find a legitimate reason for leaving his seat. He may interrupt his neighbour's work or that of his teacher with other children. There are many possible variations to the 'off-task' scenario! Similarly, if a task is too easy, children are likely to finish quickly and once again be in a position of having nothing to do — but not for long. From a management point of view, therefore, curriculum planning and the choice of appropriate tasks are the essential starting points from which all other educational setting events follow.

Records of progress

In Chapter 3 we stressed the importance of detailed and accurate records. If a teacher is indeed to keep a check on children's work and progress so that she can choose suitable activities, systematic procedures for checking work and record-keeping are essential. No-one can keep the progress and difficulties of 20–30 children in their head! Nevertheless, record-keeping requires attention to detail and both regular and frequent time commitment. The busy teacher who is concerned to prepare and conduct productive learning sessions will want a record-keeping system which places minimum demands on time, and yet contains all the necessary information for selecting appropriate activities. To this end checklists which detail teaching objectives in terms of what children will be able to do, and which also allow space for additional comments, have been found useful. We discuss developing and using records of progress in relation to children with special needs elsewhere (Solity and Bull, 1987).

Task variety

Activities can be categorised into those which are regarded as 'work', while others may be viewed as 'non-work'. Among many adults and children there is a tendency to procrastinate tasks we see as 'work', if given the chance. The less attractive or appealing a task, or the more effort it requires, the more likely we are to delay work and be distracted from it.

Gannaway (1976) illustrates the distinctions which experienced pupils (that is, of secondary age) may make between tasks, and particularly those which are made between work and non-work. When talking to pupils he found that writing was always referred to as work and was placed at the bottom of their list of preferred activities. It is likely that younger children also make discriminations between work and non-work activities and develop their own preferences. Thus activities such as story-writing and arithmetic are not often chosen ahead of painting, model-making, drama and games.

Teachers therefore need to try and find ways of presenting activities, particularly those which children find less appealing, so as to overcome pupils' initial inertia and increase their motivation. The search for interest value has resulted in many examples of inventiveness amongst teachers in order to set the occasion for on-task behaviour. However, it is difficult to be brilliantly inventive all day long and every day of the week!

We shall focus on the ways interest value can be added to tasks by making full and judicious use of the variety which is to be found within the range of educational tasks themselves. A teacher can add variety by working on the commonsense principle that 'a change is as good as a rest'. He capitalises on the differences between the tasks children are given during a lesson and throughout the day so that each activity offers some contrast with those undertaken before and after it. When planning and preparing children's work, a teacher who is concerned with variety not only considers what children are to learn from their tasks and which tasks are appropriate to their present skills and needs. He uses the dimensions on which tasks can be varied so as to incorporate interest value and sustain children's involvement. Primary teachers are well placed to plan for variety of content without the restrictions imposed on many secondary colleagues, who only work with their pupils for certain lessons and within a single curriculum area. Here then, are some of the dimensions on which you can vary children's learning activities (Table 6.1).

Table 6.1: Dimensions on which tasks can vary

Time to be spent on the task
Complexity of the task
Presentation and format
What children are to *do* during the task
Amount of pupil choice
Amount of teacher involvement
Patterns of interaction

The time to be spent on the task

Expectations as to what is a suitable length of time to spend on a task depends upon the curriculum area, the age of the children and their need for frequent changes of activity. In general, though, a teacher should be sensitive to activities which capture children's imagination and be willing to increase the length of these, while being equally responsive on occasions when an activity is not going anywhere near as well as had been hoped.

The complexity of the task

The complexity of a task may vary from a series of straightforward repetitive items to an involved problem-solving or creative activity. During the course of the school day children should be given a range of tasks which vary in their level of complexity and in the demands they make.

The presentation and format

Despite variation in content, over-frequent use of a similar format for presenting tasks, such as work-sheets, would be tedious from the children's point of view. Variety in the way work is presented is therefore essential when children are to undertake a continuous block of individual written activities.

What children are to do

Repetitions of the same kinds of behaviour during a lesson are notorious for inducing boredom, as are prolonged passive behaviours such as sitting and listening. Activities which require a combination of different behaviours are most likely to hold children's interest and keep them working for longer periods. Even seatwork activities can provide this variety: writing, reading, underlining, colouring, cutting, etc. Incorporating changes in the behaviour required is perhaps the most powerful task variable a teacher has at her disposal.

The amount of pupil choice

On some tasks children are told exactly what to do but others, for example topic work, leave them with an element of choice over what should be done and how the task can be completed. The extent to which a task involves choices by the children provides a dimension for variation. However, it needs to be stressed that where children do choose tasks they should still be told what the task entails. Where they are responsible for deciding how the task is to be completed, they should be told this too.

The amount of teacher involvement

The extent to which activities rely on teacher direction is a useful source of variety. Haring and Eaton's (1978) 'instructional hierarchy' examines different stages of teaching and the role of the teacher in facilitating learning at each stage. On some activities there is a high level of teacher direction but on others the teacher's involvement is kept to a minimum (see Solity and Bull, 1987).

Patterns of interaction

In Chapter 4 we outlined that children could be engaged in individual, cooperative or competitive working patterns, depending on the nature of the task being taught. Each of these interaction patterns has implications for seating arrangement, movement and use of materials which in themselves help provide variety across tasks.

Introducing a variety of activities to children is part and parcel of every classroom. We have discussed some, but by no means all, of the ways in which tasks can be varied and there are many different permutations and combinations, even among the examples presented here. Including variety in your plans for classroom activities will help you hold children's attention and interest, keep them busy — and avoid misbehaviour!

THE PATTERN OF ACTIVITIES

The way in which curriculum content is planned across the year and term provides the framework from which weekly and daily patterns take shape. Time is structured in progressively finer detail down through the day and its component sessions to the sequence of activities within a particular session or lesson. We concentrate here on the use of time during a single session or lesson.

Effective planning involves both selecting those activities which enable children to achieve the objectives for a session *and* ensuring that these activities can be completed in the time available. Many lesson plans which fail to work out in practice do so because of problems of timing. Too much or too little time is planned for different parts of the session; regrouping or distribution of materials takes longer than was allowed for, and so on. Effective planning therefore involves not only the selection of varied activities towards the objective for the session, but their mapping across the time available. As Marland (1975) points out, 'the pattern of the learning activities must fit both the educational aims and the stretch of time available' (p. 84).

Here we describe four important considerations when planning lessons, they are introduced in Table 6.2.

Table 6.2: Some considerations when planning lessons

Preparing a sequence of activities
Keeping the children busy
Organising concurrent activities
Thinking the plan through

Preparing a sequence of activities

It is suggested that activities be sequenced with the following issues in mind, assuming the tasks provided are appropriate to children's skills and are relevant for the objectives set.

The sequence promotes children's learning

The sequence of activities should promote the children's achievement of the particular teaching objectives in view. Thus, earlier items in the lesson should facilitate the children's performance on subsequent ones. Preliminary activities may be an orientation exercise for what is to follow.

The sequence ensures that children are actively involved

The lesson should be organised to give *every* child the opportunity to be actively involved. For example, the length and number of activities on which children are required to sit and listen (to the teacher, each other, the TV or radio) need to be decided with care. Similarly, discussion activities must be arranged so everyone can participate — and any necessary regrouping for this needs to be built into the lesson plan.

The sequence incorporates variety

A series of activities which provides variety of content, materials, behaviour and the time allowed will add interest and pace to the session. A sequence which offers contrasts between successive activities is most likely to hold the children's interest. However, it is important to bear in mind that previous activities can affect children's behaviour on their present task. Krantz and Risley (1977) showed that children's attention to the teacher or to a story book during story reading was consistently higher when this activity followed a quiet period rather than vigorous activities. Their findings question the assumption that children's attention will improve once they have 'let off steam'.

The sequence employs the 'Premack principle'

This principle may be characterised by, 'Eat up your vegetables and then you can have your ice cream'. Its classroom application involves ensuring that preferred or more exciting activities follow those which are less exciting or require more effort from the children. For example, when children have completed their individual written tasks they can progress to activities involving more interaction with their neighbours, more choice or more interesting materials. The satisfactory completion of the first task is thereby rewarded by beginning the next, more desirable, activity in the series. This makes it more likely that children will get on and finish work in time.

Keeping the children busy

The potential danger points are when children have nothing to do — and are therefore likely to fill the time with their own preferred activities and not necessarily those desired by the teacher! These danger points are most likely to occur at the start and end of a session and at the transitions between activities (Arlin, 1979). It is therefore important that these occasions are anticipated so that children always have something to keep them busy. Marland (1975) advocates the use of a *starter activity* which occupies the children right at the beginning of a lesson. He also suggests preparing *filler activities* which the teacher can use when the planned work is completed with time to spare. Becker, Englemann and Thomas (1975) describe the effective use of optional activities which children can move on to when they have satisfactorily completed a set activity ahead of their classmates. The use of preferred activities (the Premack principle) during transitions also acts as a reward for satisfactory task completion (see Chapter 7).

Organising concurrent activities

Planning sessions in which differing activities are to run at the same time can present quite a challenge to a teacher's organisational skills. To illustrate the features of preparation and planning which assist the management of concurrent activities, let us consider an example drawn from observations within a primary school.

Ms Peters had a reception class of 24 four to five-year-olds. Since they had just transferred from nursery, Ms Peters wished to provide frequent changes of task and include as much variety as possible. She felt that rotation around concurrent activities was therefore appropriate. The session observed was during an afternoon some eight weeks after the children had entered her class. Four activities were run in parallel (painting, pencil tasks, crayoning-and-cutting, number tasks). The children were grouped as usual, into their four colour-named subgroups of six children and each group was to spend approximately 20 minutes on each activity.

The different activity tables were arranged in an L-shape with the painting table near the sink, next the number table, then cutting, with pencil tasks near the door. Filler activities (lego, picture matching, dolls) were provided on the carpeted area to follow painting, which was the shortest task, or any other activity which was completed within the time available. All basic materials were laid out beforehand and children already knew where additional materials could be found (for example, puzzles, painting aprons) which were not on the tables. The sequence of events is outlined in Table 6.3.

Effective use was made during the session of visual cues, well-established routines, attention-training games and clear teacher directions (plus checking understanding). Teacher involvement centred on the pencil skills table, where Ms Peters worked with each group in turn. From here she could view the room, and in particular supervise the use of scissors on the next table. She joined each group briefly at the start and end of their activities. She gave directions on the choice and important features of their tasks and clearly stated her

Table 6.3: Example of a session involving concurrent activities

	Red group	Blue group	Green group	Yellow group
Attention routine and group directions	*Painting* Paint house (carpet-activities)	*Number puzzles* Teacher-guided choice	*Colour and cutting* Car outline prepared	*Pencil tasks* Draw picture from outing, tell sentence and copy it under teacher's model (teacher-directed)
Stop. Clear away. Table children stand behind chairs, carpet children on edge of carpet. Whole group attention game then instructions to move and groups started	*Pencil tasks* Tramline work (teacher-directed)	*Painting* House (carpet-activities)	*Number puzzles* Teacher-guided choice	*Colour and cutting* Car outline prepared
Stop. Clear away. Table children stand behind chairs, carpet children on edge of carpet. Whole group attention game then instructions to move and groups started	*Colour and cutting* Car outline prepared	*Pencil tasks* Draw vehicle (with or without templates); write or copy name (teacher-directed)	*Painting* House (carpet-activities)	*Number puzzles* Unfix cubes (bonds to ten)
Stop. Clear away. Table children stand behind chairs, carpet children on edge of carpet. Whole group attention game then instructions to move and groups started	*Number puzzles* Teacher-guided choice	*Colour and cutting* Car outline prepared	*Pencil tasks* Draw picture from outing and copywriting about picture (teacher-directed)	*Painting* House (carpet-activities)
Stop. Clear away. Table children stand behind chairs, carpet children on edge of carpet. Whole group attention game then instructions to prepare for going home				

expectations on performance, which varied both within and between groups. Finally she checked and gave immediate feedback on all completed work.

The general impression was a business-like and enjoyable session with very few queries or calls upon the teacher to correct errors or inappropriate behaviour. The key was careful planning and preparation of materials and the organisation of activities in time and space. It was also very clear that careful preparation of the children for this method of working had been undertaken in the early stages of the term!

Thinking the plan through

In planning the content, the sequence of activities, the materials and room management for any session there is always the question, 'Would this plan actually work with my pupils in my classroom?' An important step to be incorporated into the planning process is therefore to try the plan out in your imagination before trying it in the classroom! This is referred to elsewhere as a *thought experiment* (Gnagey, 1981) in which a teacher envisages the proposed session scene-by-scene as it would be 'acted out' in class. He visualises the room arrangement, the class members, the materials required and so on. Would there be sufficient pairs of scissors? How could the materials be arranged so that everyone was not converging on one point? Where would the teacher be needed at various times? How long would it take the children to clear away or regroup? What would those who finished early do whilst waiting for the others? Running such a preview of how the session would work in practice helps to anticipate hitches and difficulties that might arise. It also helps to clarify the suitability of the activities chosen to meet the objectives for the children during the session.

YOUR BEHAVIOUR IN THE TEACHING ROLE

Advanced planning and preparation helps a teacher ensure that scheduled teaching time is fully used and that children undertake appropriate, relevant and interesting learning activities. However, advanced planning is also important in setting the scene for the teacher's constructive management of children's behaviour during contact time (Glynn, 1982).

Pre-session organisation includes formulating lesson plans, arranging the room, and preparing materials and equipment so that everything needed during the lesson is to hand. Finding preparation time is not always easy, especially as most teachers have limited time during the school day, but it is nevertheless an important factor in effective teaching *and* management. Being prepared frees you to stage-manage the action once the lesson begins. It also contributes to your modelling of positive and effective work habits for children in your class to imitate!

In this final section of Chapter 6 we focus on various aspects of a teacher's verbal and non-verbal behaviour which contribute to an effective 'performance' in the teaching role. The emphasis throughout is upon communicating with pupils and sustaining their attention (Table 6.4).

Table 6.4: Communicating with pupils and sustaining their attention

Using language in class
Defining tasks for children
Asking questions
Non-verbal communication
Maintaining momentum
Keeping the children informed
Being responsive to the children

Using language in class

When giving information, explanations or directions a teacher's use of language — vocabulary, sentence structure and sequencing of content — is a major consideration. In all cases the ideas or instructions should be put clearly and fluently, using language which takes account of the age, skills and previous experiences of the children for whom they are intended.

Teachers certainly have a lot of explaining to do! A major part of their role is to enable children to understand new vocabulary, facts and, at higher levels, problems, causes, and the relationships between facts. Different types of explanation have been identified which answer differing questions (why? what? how?) and provide the basis for their preparation and presentation (see Brown and Armstrong, in Wragg, 1984). However, effective explanations will have features in common; they will need to be well-structured and clearly presented, using terms and examples which the children can understand and relate to. Thus the content and presentation of explanations should always be decided at the lesson planning stage, and prepared before the start of the lesson.

In many classrooms most interactions about educational tasks are initiated and directed by the teacher and take place within tightly structured situations. However less-structured and less teacher-directed situations, where adult and child are interacting informally during a shared activity, have been shown to have value. They facilitate children's active and spontaneous participation and assist generalisation of pupils' skills from one situation or set of materials to another (Glynn, 1982).

For further reading regarding different uses of language in teaching see Tough (1976a, 1976b, 1977), Donaldson (1978), Wells (1978) and Tizard and Hughes (1984).

Defining tasks for children

In order to set the scene for appropriate task-related behaviour, it is essential that, whatever the activity, each child understands what his task involves and how he is to go about it. The process of defining tasks for children is made easier when teaching objectives have been specified in terms of what pupils should be able to do as a result of their learning.

Pinpointing what every child needs to learn helps place the teacher in a position where she can ensure tasks are at suitable levels of difficulty and relevant to their learning. Her expectations of the children's performance will therefore be realistic. Moreover, when a series of tasks has been prepared with variety in mind, the teacher will be clear about task length, the number of items to be completed, the materials required and the behaviour expected from the children. She will also have considered the kinds of interaction that are anticipated and the level of her own involvement during the activity.

She is undertaking a process which parallels the definition of acceptable classroom behaviour outlined in Chapter 5, by clarifying what tasks a lesson involves. The teacher is then in a position to communicate her expectations and activity-based rules as clearly as she does her rules for classroom behaviour (see Medland and Vitale, 1984). This investment in preparation prepares the way for good communication between teacher and children during contact time. It contributes to a shared understanding of what tasks involve and what the expectations of the children actually are.

93

Gnagey (1981) points out the use of pupil accountability as a factor in sustaining their performance. However, if children are to be accountable for what they do, teachers must be accountable for both setting appropriate tasks and also making the task requirements crystal clear.

Brophy and Evertson (1976) suggest three types of information which facilitate children's progress on educational tasks:

(1) what task is to be completed;
(2) where help is to be found if needed;
(3) that finished work will be checked by the teacher.

Other task-related features can be added to these, and the full list is shown in Table 6.5.

Asking questions

Teacher questions serve many functions and indeed a teacher may have several reasons for asking a particular question at a certain time. As with explanations, it is important that questions are planned, necessary and relevant to pupils' learning. Questions must be framed in the context of the lesson and their purpose must be clear to the teacher before they are put to the children! Some functions of questions are shown in Table 6.6.

Depending on their function, questions will be directed towards individuals, small groups or to the class as a whole. They may even be intended to elicit a mass response from the group, in which case formats requiring brief answers would be preferable!

When used to sustain attention, teachers often give a general question and then add an individual's name, for example, 'How many legs does a spider have?', pause, '— Sophie'. This format gets everyone thinking, rather than just the child towards whom the question is addressed. When directing questions to individuals it is important to recall the insidious effects of location, since where children sit can determine the number of questions they are asked (Moore, 1980, 1982). Some teachers use a pack of name cards when questioning in group situations, such as quizzes. They call on the child whose name is on top and then place his card at the bottom so that everyone has a turn. This is just one, elaborate but certain way of overcoming location and positional effects.

Teachers use differing types of question, depending on their

Table 6.5: Defining tasks for the children: what they need to know.

'I keep six honest serving men/They taught me all I knew:/Their names are What and Why and When/And How and Where and Who'. Rudyard Kipling (from Peter, 1977)

Information children need	Points to be included
What they are to do	The type of task. Exactly what to do, for example, write, cut, talk, etc. How much they are to do. The amount of choice in the task. And what to do when they have finished; for example, bring your work to the teacher, or raise your hand, or put your book in a collection place. Whether to go on to another activity (specified) or to tidy away.
Why they are doing it	The purpose of the task, for example, to practise addition; to discover which, among a group of objects, float and sink — and why; the important features which the teacher will look for, for example, accuracy, speed of working, number of different solutions to a particular problem.
When they are to start and finish	The part of the lesson. The length of time that will be allowed for the task.
How they are to get help	Whether they are to ask the teacher, partner or group. How to seek the teacher's attention, for example put up your hand or bring work to teacher.
Where they are to work	The part of the school or base. The seating arrangement — fixed or choice. The movement which is allowed.
Who will work with them	Whether they are to work alone, or with a partner or group. Their interaction — cooperative or competitive.

Table 6.6: Some functions of questions

> To get the children thinking
> To revise or recall previous information or skills
> To structure a task
> To arouse curiosity or interest
> To draw on pupils' own experiences, views and feelings
> To check understanding
> To diagnose children's difficulties
> To stimulate questions and discussion among pupils
> To encourage participation by shy or reluctant children
> To express interest in pupils' ideas or feelings
> To gain attention and keep children 'on-task'

purpose and context and the children to whom they are addressed. Questions of the same or different type may be used together in a sequence. For example, open questions may lead into more specific ones or several questions may be asked which seek examples of a principle already given in the lesson.

In brief the essentials of effective questioning would seem to be:

(1) Their purpose, type and timing are worked out at the lesson planning stage.
(2) Their length and structure are such that they will be understood by children for whom they are intended.
(3) Only one question is asked at a time
(4) They are arranged in a logical sequence which is relevant to the learning task.
(5) Individual questions are evenly but randomly distributed around the group.
(6) They are addressed to *children* (rather than the back wall or blackboard!) and can be heard by all those involved.

Dealing with children's answers to questions is, of course, as important as the questions themselves. Children's willingness to contribute should be acknowledged and praised even if they are not ultimately called upon to answer the question. It is important to give a child sufficient time to respond to a question and to make sure that everyone who needs to hear his answer does so, repeating it for them when necessary.

Handling 'wrong' answers is a particularly sensitive area for teacher and child, especially when these occur within a group or class. When children do not answer questions correctly they may be unintentionally punished by their teacher's reaction. A pause or change in facial expression can be sufficient to make some children feel foolish and embarrassed. There is a need then, to create an atmosphere in which contributions are welcomed and mistakes are accepted by teacher and pupils alike. Beware, too, of accepting only the answer you expect. You may otherwise discount answers that are well thought out and useful contributions. Children can sometimes 'put it better' than you can yourself.

General advice on dealing with 'wrong' answers is offered by Marland (1975):

Never mind. Use them for what they are — next steps to further thought — and take up the answer as a challenge for you to devise rapidly the next appropriate question. Never, or almost never, ridicule, but turn the answer to good account. It will be a guide to the pupil's misunderstanding. Don't labour the point. Explain a confusion. If there has been a misunderstanding, ask the question which clears it . . .' (p. 76)

Non-verbal communication

Just as non-verbal behaviour assists a teacher in conveying leadership, so it has been shown to be significant in the teacher role, notably by communicating enthusiasm and sustaining attention.

A common experience of school children, which you may recall from your own school days, if that of enjoying subjects which the teacher seems to enjoy. Boring subjects are often those which are presented in a boring way by a teacher who conveys little interest or enthusiasm. Somehow enthusiasm, or the lack of it, is communicated from the teacher to pupils. In a similar way a public speaker, colleague or chance acquaintance succeeds or fails to hold our attention and interest. Robertson (1981) examines in detail the characteristic ways in which enthusiasm is, or is not, communicated. His analysis once again highlights the all-important influence of non-verbal behaviour in supporting and emphasising the verbal message, drawing our attention to what is said — or alternatively, detracting from it.

As in the role of leader, a teacher must therefore look to his *total* communication, and not rely solely on getting the verbal message right. However, the important corollary to Robertson's analysis (which we would recommend to you) is that one cannot work on the communication of enthusiasm and hence holding attention merely by practising the appropriate accompanying gestures, voice tone and so on. The effect would then only resemble an inept actor's attempts to communicate his dramatic role. The teacher most effectively communicates his enthusiasm by becoming involved and interested in the verbal content himself. Through his own involvement and interest in what is being presented, the non-verbal elements of communication will be successfully integrated with, and support, the verbal message. You may communicate the verbal message effectively *without* personal enthusiasm but the 'non-verbals' will give you away. The implication is clear: to sustain pupils' attention and involvement over successive tasks, days and weeks — sustain your own!

Maintaining momentum

The pace at which lessons are conducted varies across the school day and between sessions. It can be planned in advance and built into the sequence of daily activities. However, the pace at which lessons run depends partly upon the teacher's own behaviour. Gnagey (1981) cites work by Kounin (1970) who found from observational research in classrooms that pupil misbehaviours were markedly fewer when lessons moved at an optimal pace. This was regarded as being fast enough to sustain attention and interest but not so fast as to lose pupils along the way.

Kounin has identified some of the ways in which teacher behaviour can inadvertently interrupt or slow down the pace of activities and leave room for misbehaviours. A teacher may dwell upon a small misdemeanour at great length to the discomfort and boredom of the group. Similarly when a teacher reacts to every little action by her pupils (dropping a ruler, sneezing, movement of a chair, a whisper and so on) she succeeds only in enlarging the minor instances. Through her *own* behaviour the session is unnecessarily punctuated by irrelevant events which would otherwise pass unnoticed. Another source of interruption to a session's flow is the teacher's use of instructions about the task which are too long and complicated.

In short, any action by the teacher which distracts the attention of children and herself away from the main purpose of the activities or the session, or which provides sections of the group with 'do nothing time', will interrupt the pace of the session and invite undesired behaviour from the children. Many interruptions of the kinds mentioned can be prevented through careful planning. Decisions can be taken about which parts of the session require most emphasis, which materials or equipment need explanation, what explanations are necessary for different tasks and so on. Thinking the plan through beforehand helps you to identify ways in which group tasks can be managed so as to avoid fragmentation. It can also highlight points at which you may be in danger of digressing to interesting, but less relevant issues.

Keeping the children informed

Children are most likely to feel fully involved in a lesson when they are given details of the shape of the session: the range and purpose of activities to be undertaken. Otherwise they may experience just a series of activities, the relationship between which is unclear. Marland (1975) describes how the teacher can provide 'signposts' by telling the children the direction of the lesson at the outset and at intervals during its course. He also suggests a final 'arrival board' or joint summing-up during which the teacher can give the group feedback so they can appreciate what they have achieved. Giving advance markers about time keeps the children informed as to how they are progressing towards finishing their tasks and how much needs to be completed in the remaining time available. Advance markers also prepare pupils for a change of activity.

Being responsive to the children

The final aspect of the teacher's performance to be considered here concerns sensitivity to the group and to the individuals within it. Once again the importance of planning and preparation needs to be emphasised in this context. When a teacher is sure where he and his pupils are going, when the preparatory organisation is complete, he is free to communicate effectively, not only *to* the group but also *with* the group.

The teacher can then concentrate on monitoring children's reactions to what he says and to their tasks. He can be alert to their signals of interest, boredom and non-comprehension and he can respond to them. He can regulate the pace and course of the lesson and is able to make corrections to both when needed.

A well-planned or indeed 'scripted' lesson in which content, organisation and timing are prepared in detail need not, in our view, be restrictive nor reduce opportunities for spontaneity. We would argue that paradoxically the structure can free you from concentrating on the nuts and bolts of the session: a case of 'science freeing the art'. You then would be able to adopt a more relaxed approach so that ad-libbing, humour and spontaneity can also develop during your lessons.

Responsiveness involves taking an active interest in the children and what they are doing. It also involves a willingness to act upon children's reactions and to be flexible: to change the task, to take time to explain, to allow a stimulating topic to continue a little longer whilst interest remains high. It is the mechanism by which a well-planned presentation is translated into a three-way pattern of interaction: between teacher, children and their tasks.

SUMMARY

In Chapter 6 we discussed aspects of the teaching role in managing the educational setting events for children's behaviour in class.

First we considered the teacher's selection of educational tasks which children will undertake in his lessons. When he sets curricular tasks at suitable levels of difficulty, and includes variety in the activities he plans, the teacher helps pupils to start work, keep working — and enjoy their learning activities.

Effective planning involves not only selecting those activities from which children will learn, but mapping them across the time available in each teaching session during the course of the school year. In the context of lesson planning, we discussed the sequencing of activities; keeping children busy during transitions *between* activities; organising concurrent activities and thinking the plan through. Taking these considerations into account helps ensure that teaching time is fully used and that lessons run smoothly.

Advanced planning and preparation also set the scene for effective teaching and management once lessons begin. In the final section of Chapter 6 we considered important aspects of a teacher's verbal and non-verbal behaviour in the teaching role. We examined the teacher's use of language in class, in particular when giving presentations, explaining tasks and asking questions. We described how a teacher communicates enthusiasm and holds pupils' attention through his non-verbal behaviour. Finally we outlined how a teacher can carry the children *with* him through a lesson by maintaining momentum, keeping them informed and being responsive to their reactions and needs.

Part Three

Working out the Consequences

7

When They Are 'Good'

INTRODUCTION

We now move from the management of setting events within the classroom environment and focus upon the management of consequences which follow children's behaviour.

A teacher who is operating a positive system of management is primarily concerned with children's desirable behaviours: setting up the classroom situation so as to facilitate these from the children and providing consequences which confirm their responses as appropriate. It is therefore towards the consequences for desired or appropriate behaviour that we direct our attention first. In this chapter we begin by considering the essential ingredients of consequences which a teacher uses to strengthen behaviour: feedback and reinforcers. Then we outline the different types of reward which can be effective as reinforcers with children. In Chapter 8 we shall go on to discuss their selection and use in class.

INCREASING (STRENGTHENING) BEHAVIOUR

Consequences which strengthen children's appropriate behaviour are those which are pleasant or desirable from the children's point of view. Such pleasant consequences make it more likely that the children will behave in this way again in response to similar circumstances.

Children may derive pleasant outcomes directly from their behaviour itself, for example the satisfaction of completing their work. However, very many of the consequences they receive for classroom behaviour are provided by their teacher. For instance the end-of-break bell rings and the classgroup file quickly and quietly into class and to their places; their teacher praises them for doing so. His praise serves two purposes. It confirms that this behaviour in response to the end-of-break bell is what he wants, and if the children like his praise then he is also making it more likely that they will respond to the end-of-break bell in a similar way in future.

In order to serve this dual purpose effectively, consequences provided by the teacher often combine two elements. These are *feedback* (knowledge of results as to what the children did which was appropriate) and a *reinforcer* (a pleasant event).

Feedback (knowledge of results)

As children (and adults) we are not always aware of the behaviour we show, nor do we always notice the consequences of our behaviour in response to particular circumstances. Occasionally when learning new behaviour, we may notice that we obtained the outcome we desired but without realising what we did that was appropriate.

When a teacher provides feedback to children she helps them to overcome these difficulties by establishing these connections for them. She may point out that a behaviour was appropriate and what the behaviour was: 'That's right, blue group, you have all put your books in neat piles'. She may underline the links between a behaviour and its consequences: 'Now you can read all the new words for book 5, you can start book 5's story'; 'You have all finished your work in time so we can have our five-minute quiz'. Alternatively, a teacher may link the children's correct behaviour back to the setting events: 'Well done, class 5 you've all remembered the 'Save Energy' campaign and closed the door each time today'. Important among these setting events are rules: 'Good, John, you've remembered our rule about working hard and letting others get on'. These variations in feedback all point out which behaviour the children showed that was desirable. Some link it to its consequences, others to the relevant cues in the setting events. Of course, one might link the behaviour to both its setting events and consequences simultaneously. For instance, in the last example the teacher might have also referred to the consequences for John: 'You'll soon have your writing finished and be ready to draw your picture'.

By pointing out appropriate behaviour and its links to circumstances and outcomes, the teacher enables the children to be more aware of their own behaviour and to make these links for themselves more quickly than they would alone. Feedback is therefore crucial when teaching new skills, be they academic or social, in helping children to see how well they are doing and what improvement they have made. During the early stages of learning new behaviour it is not easy for them to judge when they are getting it right. By providing feedback for the children the teacher helps them to see their behaviour and their progress for themselves. Later on she can ask the children to make such comments about their own performance and social behaviour, and even to comment occasionally on each other's appropriate behaviour. Such comments by the children will provide checks for the teacher to see that pupils are beginning to make the connections for themselves. Learning that things do not merely happen by chance or fate, that their actions have effects, will assist children's progress towards monitoring and regulating their own behaviour.

Reinforcers

Consequences which we find desirable, and increase the likelihood that we will behave in a particular way again, are called *reinforcers*. The obvious pleasant consequences which lead us, as adults, to repeat behaviours include feedback of success and achievement alone; the smiles, pleasant words and actions of other people; and the pay we receive each week or month. However, we are also likely to continue to behave in ways which enable us to avoid or to stop less pleasant events, for these behaviours also result in desirable outcomes. For example, we take care to protect ourselves when handling hot objects in the kitchen, when the TV is too loud we turn it down, and we avoid or limit our contact with acquaintances we dislike.

Of course, what one person finds pleasant another may not. This is a particularly important consideration when a teacher is providing consequences for good work and behaviour in class. Some children may continue to work hard at their tasks for teacher praise, whilst others may respond better to house points or to high marks for their good performance. Similarly, pupils may seek to *avoid* different events. Thus, whilst Gary may work feverishly to complete his task in order to avoid *missing* the end of morning quiz, Emma may prefer not to join in the quiz. She may seek to avoid this by working slowly and having unfinished work to complete during quiztime.

There are many events which can be said to be reinforcing for most children of a particular age, for example, adult attention, hugs, badges or sweets for young children. However, we cannot simply *assume* that a particular thing or event will reinforce the behaviour of a child.

It is only by getting to know the children well, observing what they choose and avoid, what they work for and what they do not, and finding out from them what they enjoy, that you can establish which events may be effective reinforcers for the children in your class group. The real test would be to try something which you judge to be suitable as a reinforcer and see what happens. If the behaviour which it follows occurs more often over a period of time, this consequence is indeed reinforcing. If there is no change or the behaviour occurs less often, the consequence is not acting as a reinforcer.

Any behaviour is strengthened and increased when it is followed by events which are pleasant from the child's point of view. Unfortunately this means we can unintentionally strengthen undesired as well as desired behaviour. For example, a mother may give her toddler sweets to quieten him, particularly if he is crying loudly in a public place. He will probably stop crying to eat his sweets, but if he likes sweets they serve only to strengthen his undesirable behaviour, making it more likely that he will cry in public places in future (Table 7.1).

Table 7.1: Strengthening undesired behaviour: what the child learns at the checkout

Setting events	Child's behaviour	Consequences
Supermarket checkout, mother unloading the trolley	Loud crying	Mother gives him sweets
Child learns: To cry loudly at the supermarket checkout		

Incidentally, you will note that his mother in her turn is reinforced for giving him sweets, since the crying stops. Giving her toddler sweets stops an event which is unpleasant for her and she will be more likely to use this when he cries in this situation in future (Table 7.2)

As we pointed out in Chapter 2, undesired behaviour in the classroom is equally subject to unintentional reinforcement — particularly in the form of attention from the teacher or from classmates!

Table 7.2: Strengthening undesired behaviour: what the mother learns at the checkout

Setting events	Mother's behaviour	Consequences
Supermarket checkout, child crying loudly	Gives him sweets	Child's crying stops
Mother learns: To give her child sweets when he cries at the checkout		

Intrinsic and extrinsic reinforcers

School children of any age are accomplished at many behaviours, which are already reinforced and maintained by consequences *intrinsic* to the behaviour itself. These behaviours are maintained simply because completing them successfully is found desirable or satisfying by the children. This is the goal we are working towards with all aspects of their academic and social behaviour at school. We hope the children will derive satisfaction and pleasure from completing their work and making progress. We would like them to value learning for its own sake. However, children are introduced to new educational and social skills throughout their schooling. Many of these are complex, and for a large number of children it will take some time to achieve the competence necessary for intrinsic consequences to occur. Let us illustrate this by comparing two children's behaviour.

The first is a child of whom we would say 'He enjoys reading'. There are several observations which might lead us to this conclusion: the amount of time he spends reading, his frequent requests to take books home, his descriptions of stories he has read, and so on. For him, reading brings about its own reinforcers. He finds satisfaction in being able to read and amusement in the stories he reads; he can find out new information about his interests. His competence at reading is such that his reading behaviour is strengthened and maintained by these *intrinsic* reinforcers which follow directly from the behaviour itself.

A second child is unwilling to share crayons with others at his table. We can readily understand that sharing might not be intrinsically reinforcing since from the child's point of view he is worse off. Instead of having the crayons he needs as and when he wants them, he must ask for them and wait for them to be returned or use other colours. In the absence of intrinsic reinforcers, another source of reinforcement is necessary in order to encourage him to share. His teacher may provide this by praising him: providing external or *extrinsic* reinforcement. By pointing out his desired behaviour and

107

the benefits of sharing, she also provides feedback. The long-term goal of treating sharing in this way is that ultimately the child will gain *intrinsic satisfaction* from sharing.

When associated with a pleasant event, such as praise, eventually feedback itself will come to be valued by children. It is then more likely that their behaviour will become strengthened by their own recognition that they have behaved appropriately, or made some progress in their work. In this way feedback from the teacher helps children to derive intrinsic reinforcement from their activities even before the ultimate aim of competence is achieved.

The teacher's direct part in providing external sources of feedback and reinforcement obviously becomes less important as children's awareness of their own behaviour increases and as their behaviour is maintained by intrinsic reinforcers. The way is then prepared for children to monitor and regulate their own behaviour, without the need for mediation by their teacher. We shall look at this stage in Chapter 11.

Reinforcers, rewards and bribery!

The terms 'extrinsic reinforcers' and 'rewards' are often confused. Let us explain the difference between them and then discuss some possible misgivings which may be associated with 'rewards'.

Reinforcers are consequences for which we have confirmatory evidence that they actually work. That is, they are known to increase or to maintain the particular behaviour they follow. Rewards, on the other hand, are a 'best guess' at what events or things may act as reinforcers for particular children. For example we might anticipate that many young children value teacher praise or stars and so use these as rewards in class. However, until we can confirm that these rewards do indeed increase or maintain the behaviour they follow, we cannot say they *are* reinforcers.

There is, we find, a tendency among parents and teachers to resist the use of rewards as being somehow equivalent to 'bribery' with all the negative connotations which that term carries. We would point out the differences at the outset. First, there are significant differences in timing. A bribe is often given before the behaviour; whereas rewards *always* follow the behaviour. They are consequences and must always be earned before they are given; whereas bribes are often given in the hope that they will be earned. Secondly, there are major differences in purpose. Bribes are used to persuade others to do things which are known to be unacceptable or even, perhaps, illegal. The use of rewards in classroom management is directed towards strengthening behaviour which is socially acceptable in class and which assists the children's learning on educational tasks.

A further common misconception about rewards is that they must be tangible, such as sweets, money or prizes of some kind. This naturally leads to worries about the cost of providing rewards for a family or classgroup, and fears that by using rewards one is teaching children to do things for material gain only. Such fears would indeed by justified if rewards did only include material goods. However, there are several types of reward of which the tangible varieties comprise only one. Such 'material' rewards are selected only when other types are considered ineffective or inappropriate for particular children. The choice among rewards is discussed fully later. At this point we would just establish the fact that material, tangible rewards need not, and indeed must not, be the only type available.

Finally teachers and parents have expressed disquiet at the use of rewards as somehow unnatural or artificial. In fact, rewards play a very natural part in our everyday lives. We return a friend's greeting with a smile, we thank someone for their help and we give compliments. Parents play with their children, show them affection and provide them with access to a range of pleasant activities and treats of various kinds.

So, too, rewards occur as a natural part of children's experience in school. In particular we might think of the spontaneous reactions by teachers and others to children's desirable social behaviour and progress. However, many rewards which occur in school are deliberately arranged by teachers. Examples include the pattern of activities in which seat-work is followed by, perhaps, artwork or science activities; the comments which a teacher puts on a page of 'good' work; the selection of one group to go out to play first because they are ready quickly. To the extent that they are used deliberately and systematically, these rewards may be seen as 'artificial'. Nevertheless, they *are* natural everyday events within the context of school settings. For reasons we shall explain later, it is crucial that a teacher arranges as many such rewards as possible within the natural pattern of events in class.

TYPES OF REWARD

Here we describe four types of reward which a teacher might use in conjunction with feedback to strengthen children's appropriate

109

behaviour. Which of these will be effective reinforcers for particular children will depend on a number of factors, elaborated in Chapter 8.

Social rewards

These involve pleasant interactions with other people, adults or children. Examples would include teacher praise, smiles and feedback, opportunities to sit with friends or to show good work to the headteacher. For very young children, physical contact, such as a hug, ruffling or stroking the hair, is also very rewarding. Many appropriate social behaviours are strengthened and maintained by the behaviours of others; these are their natural consequences.

For most children social rewards, particularly adult attention and praise, are very powerful. However, there are some children for whom social interactions may not already be reinforcing. Moreover when children meet a new teacher, they may have little or no experience of him and may not yet value him as a source of approval. Where social rewards are not yet reinforcing for some children it is necessary to find other events which *are* already known to be motivating for these children, and to use these, coupled with praise. Other types of reward are also very useful when a teacher wishes to provide a variety and range of rewards in class (see Chapter 8).

Activity rewards

These may be arranged as part of the natural sequence of classroom activities, as we outlined in Chapter 6. However, they include any activity which children enjoy. Thus a teacher might arrange a free choice interval between parts of a teaching session. She may even agree to a child sharpening all his group's pencils after he has completed his work — if this is what he *really* would like to do. Activity rewards are only reinforcing in so far as they are those the *children* enjoy.

Token rewards

These are more tangible signs of success or approval. Stars may be stuck in children's books or on a wall chart; badges may be given worn

to wear for the day, or points may be given for remembering to follow classroom routines. Tokens are useful as they can be given immediately and can even be exchanged for other rewards later on. In the latter case, they can save time and organisation in delivery and keep their value through the access they provide to other rewards. They also act as a link from the desired behaviour to a delayed reward such as a period of free activity choice at the end of the session or day. An example of such a system in use is given on p. 147.

Material rewards

In some cases it may be difficult to find events which are reinforcing for particular children. For example, very young entrants to school may have little experience of contact with other children or unfamiliar adults so that social rewards may not, at first be suitable. Moreover, some may have limited experience of the play activities available and stars and stickers may not yet have acquired any value. Material rewards, the most tangible of all, may therefore be necessary with these young children and, perhaps, with older youngsters whose previous experience has not taught them to value the more usual rewards available in school. Material rewards include 'consumables' of all kinds: sweets, trinkets, toys and so on. Used on an everyday basis, or with older children, this type of reward would be perhaps the least natural of all rewards occurring in school. They seem more likely to be reserved for commendation of excellence including, as they do, prizes of all kinds!

Whenever so-called 'back-up' rewards, such as specially arranged activities or material rewards, are used it is essential that they are *always* paired with a more naturally occurring event, such as praise, *and* with feedback. The intention here is that through their association with more tangible and (currently) rewarding events, the reward-value of these more natural school events such as teacher praise, house points and so on will be increased. Once these other types of reward are well established as reinforcing for the children's behaviour, the back-up rewards can and must be gradually withdrawn. Similarly by pairing rewards with knowledge of results it is the intention, as we have mentioned, that the feedback of success and achievement in itself will become motivating. In this way it is hoped that eventually children will keep working because of the consequences which are intrinsic to their tasks, rather than solely because of encouragement received from a particular teacher.

always pair material reward with praise.

These different types of reward, together with classroom examples, are shown in Table 7.3.

Table 7.3: Types of reward and some classroom examples

Type	Main features	Examples	Comments
Social rewards	Involve pleasant interactions with other people	Praise, applause, the opportunity to sit with friends or show good work to favourite teacher. Touch, hugs (young children). Smiles. A written note to parents about good progress or behaviour	They are determined by the behaviour of others. Often the natural consequence of social behaviours
Activity rewards	Involve opportunities for enjoyable activities	Any preferred activity: play as individual or group; games; read to the teacher; clean board; work on topic of interest; free choice of activity, etc	The activity offered must be the *child's* preferred activity. It is best to avoid curricular activities. May also involve social reinforcers e.g. playing a group game with friends
Token rewards	Visual, tangible signs of approval or progress	Stars, points, grades, ticks, badges, merit cards, certificates	These can be used alone or exchanged for activity or material rewards later: they are easier to arrange immediately
Material rewards	Tangible/usable/edible items	Sweets, playthings, trinkets and prizes or presents of all kinds	These are generally reserved for use as a back-up *only* with very young children or when all other types are ineffective. Always pair these with other types of reward to strengthen the efffectiveness of the new reward.

SUMMARY

In Chapter 7 we have introduced consequences which strengthen a behaviour, making it more likely that children will behave in this way in future. Some behaviours are strengthened by pleasant outcomes which follow directly from the behaviour itself: intrinsic reinforcers. However, in class children will more often need the feedback and reinforcers their teacher arranges for them in order to learn and maintain new behaviours.

What is pleasant for some children may not be so for others. So, it is important that you provide suitable rewards that you can anticipate will indeed act as reinforcers and strengthen the children's appropriate behaviour. We have outlined four types: social, activity, token and material rewards.

When using rewards together with feedback you are confirming for your pupils that they *are* 'being good' and in what ways. You are also encouraging them to 'be good' in future. The intention in using these consequences for appropriate behaviour is that ultimately children will become more aware of their own appropriate behaviour and its outcomes. They can then begin to gain intrinsic satisfaction from their work and social interactions.

How can you apply all this to your situation? Which rewards are likely to work for you and your pupils? How can you set up a really effective pattern of consequences to encourage and maintain 'good' behaviour? These are issues we address in the next chapter.

8

Working on the Positives

INTRODUCTION

Directly or indirectly a teacher influences the majority of consequences her pupils receive for behaving appropriately in class. This chapter is concerned with the effective management of these consequences so as to get 'good' behaviour established and keep the children behaving in the ways desired.

Once again we highlight the importance of careful preparation. We suggest ways in which you can prepare *yourself* so as to maximise your success. We discuss the consequences you might arrange, emphasising the value of your own praise and offering guidelines for choosing other rewards. We go on to consider how to make the most effective use of these positive consequences in strengthening and maintaining 'good' behaviour. Finally we describe sources of rewards for your pupils other than those you give personally. Included here are achievements they can find in their work and the encouragement which other people can offer them.

PREPARING THE WAY

Effective management of consequences in the classroom relies upon: a teacher's success in defining for herself and for her pupils those behaviours which are wanted; her arrangement of suitable consequences and her consistent use of them.

How then can you prepare to manage consequences effectively? We would identify four elements which contribute to a teacher's success:

(1) clearly defining 'good' behaviour,
(2) being free to notice children's behaviour,
(3) being willing to acknowledge the 'ordinary',
(4) being prepared to arrange suitable consequences and to follow them through.

Clearly defining 'good' behaviour

The behavioural approach, with its fundamental concern with observable events, provides the basis for clear definitions as to which behaviours are desirable in particular circumstances. 'Good' behaviours are therefore defined in terms which make observations easy and consistent with different children, across various settings and over time. It is, for example, easier to spot children who are 'writing' than those who are 'getting on'.

When the teacher has formulated a set of rules for classroom behaviour, she has already spelled out for herself and her pupils which appropriate behaviours she will be looking for. Especially in the early stages, she will be giving frequent reminders to the children — and herself — as to which behaviours are desired. Similarly, when the requirements of children's learning tasks have been clearly defined the teacher can be certain about what behaviours to look for as children set about their work. Clearly specified rules and educational tasks help teachers to communicate effectively to pupils so the children know where they stand and what is expected. They also automatically set the scene for a teacher to 'catch children being good' because she knows what 'good' means in terms of how the children should behave.

Being free to notice children's behaviour

We have already emphasised the importance of planning and preparation in freeing the teacher during contact time so that he can be *in* contact with the children and alert to the responses of individuals and groups during the course of the session. There is no way that a teacher can be in minute-by-minute personal contact with all his pupils. However, there is a need to monitor their behaviour frequently, even if from the far end of the room. There is little point in having clear expectations as to how the children should behave unless their appropriate behaviours can be seen and acted upon!

The traditional classroom seating arrangement, using rows with the teacher placed front and centre, would seem to assist the teacher in monitoring children's behaviour during certian kinds of seatwork (Glynn, 1982). However, as outlined in Chapter 4, there are many activities for which rows would not be the most appropriate choice of seating and most seating arrangements present difficulties of monitoring from a single position. Whichever arrangement is chosen, the teacher will need to move around the room and scan it often and from different viewpoints to monitor the children's behaviour effectively. His attention can easily become monopolised when attending to an individual or subgroup, and the rest of the class can also become screened from sight. It is obvious therefore that at these times he must position himself so that he can always keep 'one eye' on the rest of the group without needing to turn around or peer over the queue of children which has gathered around him!

By knowing which behaviours to look for and by ensuring you are free to scan the room frequently, regardless of what you yourself are doing, the task of monitoring children's behaviour and therefore of consequence management is made easier.

Being willing to acknowledge the 'ordinary'

A willingness to acknowledge and act upon ordinary acceptable behaviours plays a crucial part in consequence management. Acceptable behaviours in class tend to be less noticeable and receive less attention than misbehaviours, perhaps for a number of reasons. First, unwanted behaviours often involve more movement and noise than their acceptable counterparts. Secondly, unwanted behaviours often interrupt the session so a teacher is more likely to be sensitive and alert to these than to behaviours which facilitate a smooth-running lesson. Thirdly, acceptable behaviours are only those which are expected from the children anyway. So we may well feel disinclined to be other than neutral in our reaction to these. The underlying and often incorrect assumption here is that the children intuitively share the teacher's expectations of their behaviour in class, without the need to make these expectations explicit.

There is also the unease that commenting on the ordinary will lead children to 'rest on their laurels' rather than trying to improve. Finally, it would seem to be almost human nature to leave things alone when they are going well, intervening only when they have gone wrong. This is a common feature of child management in a variety of situations. For example, a parent may leave the children when they are playing well, returning if a quarrel begins; a teacher may seize the opportunity to work with a small group, or hear a child read once the class group has settled to work, intervening only when troublesome behaviour occurs. The management of adults follows similar tendencies: a superior is more likely to initiate contact with a member of his staff when an error or problem has occurred than when things are just running smoothly!

The teacher concerned with positive management must be aware of these predispositions to overlook acceptable behaviours, and deliberately look out for their occurrence, so that she can indeed 'catch the children being good'. Here again we see the value of positive classroom and activity-based rules. They help to highlight and attract a teacher's attention to behaviours she might otherwise take for granted.

Being prepared to arrange consequences and to follow them through

There remains the question of what to *do* about children's behaviour in class. It is necessary for a teacher to clarify in advance what consequences children can receive for their good behaviours, when these will happen and how they will be arranged. These decisions constitute the final stage in preparing for consequence management and we can therefore now consider in some detail the choice of consequences for desirable behaviour.

When thinking up rewards to use in your classroom there are at least three important considerations. First, you will need to find rewards which are most likely to appeal to, and be effective with, your particular group of children. Rewards should therefore be chosen with their ages and interests in mind. Secondly, the rewards you choose must be those which you can make available and organise relatively easily. Last, but by no means least, you will wish to choose rewards that *you* are comfortable with and can give in a relaxed and natural way.

Perhaps the most powerful reward that you have at your disposal is your own approval. Your approval, expressed through praise, smiles etc., plays a crucial part in fostering a positive classroom atmosphere — and you as well as your pupils will gain from this. We therefore explain the effective use of praise before going on to outline the choice of other rewards.

117

EFFECTIVE PRAISE

There is more to praise than just saying 'Well done'. Both *what* is said and *how* it is said contribute to the effectiveness of praise in strengthening 'good' behaviour. Here we outline full praise statements, shorter (partial) statements and ways in which effective praise is given.

Full praise statements

There are as many as five separate steps in a full statement of praise, which we introduce in Table 8.1 (see also Medland and Vitale, 1984). These include feedback together with references to the setting events and possible consequences.

Table 8.1: Steps in a full praise statement

Step 1:	Gain attention and show approval
Step 2:	Say why you are pleased
Step 3:	Say what progress or improvement there has been
Step 4:	Mention other consequences which may follow
Step 5:	Give a motivational challenge

Step 1: gain attention and show approval

Clearly, praise would be in vain if the children concerned were unaware of it! So it is crucial to make sure they are named individually or as a group and that you have their attention. It is equally important that they know a *praise* statement is being made. Therefore the first words should convey approval, for example, 'Well done, Jimmy'; 'Yes, group two, that's right'.

Step 2: say why you are pleased

Next it is important to give feedback: saying exactly what the children have done that is pleasing. Wherever possible, the teacher specifies the appropriate behaviour or what children have achieved. By using social or activity-based rules, feedback is made easier since the teacher's words can simply echo the rules: for example, 'You've remembered to use capitals and full stops'; 'You are all looking and listening carefully'. This part of the praise statement underlines the match between the behaviour and its setting events. At the same time it can serve to clarify and remind children of the rule.

Step 3: say what progress there has been

It is often helpful to highlight the improvement noticed over a period of time, particularly when working on new or weak behaviours. For instance it may be the second day running that the group has entered the room and taken their places quietly. It may be the third time today that Sean has been ready to start work with all the materials he needs. The teacher says so at this point.

Step 4: mention other possible consequences

Whilst praise is the immediate reward, other outcomes are possible. Thus a teacher might refer to the natural consequences of the appropriate behaviour, for example, 'Keep this up and you'll be really good at spelling'. Alternatively the other outcomes may be specially arranged: 'You'll be finished in time to choose what you do for the last five minutes of the lesson'; 'Your mum will be pleased when I tell her'; 'You've earned a star on your chart'.

Step 5: give a motivational challenge

The final phrase presents the child or group with a challenge which is intended to encourage them to keep trying, for example, 'Do you think you can do that again?', 'Can you try as hard tomorrow?'. Whether or not the child answers 'Yes', their teacher has the opportunity to express personal confidence by adding a phrase such as 'Well, I think you can'.

Table 8.2 shows some examples of full praise statements with each of these five steps numbered. The statements are placed in the context of the setting event and behaviour to which they refer.

Full praise statements are particularly necessary when working to establish new or weak behaviours. However they are too lengthy, of course, to be used every time. They could be disruptive to the lesson or distract children's attention from their work. None the less, it is important to use them as often as possible during a lesson with individuals, groups and the whole class. At a minimum they should be given to the class early in the session, in the middle and at the end.

Table 8.2: Some examples of full praise statements

Example	*Setting event*	*Behaviour*
1	The rule is to finish work (in the time given)	The children all complete their work in time

Praise statement

(1) Well done, Class 3! (2) You've all finished your work in the time, (3) and that's the second time today. (4) Keep this up and there'll be time for free choice later on. (5) Do you think you can finish all today's work in time? . . . Yes? . . . So do I.

Example	*Setting event*	*Behaviour*
2	The class rule is to be friendly and helpful	Darren takes turns on the Language Master without complaining or pushing

Praise statement

(1) Darren, I'm pleased to see (2) you taking you're turn, that's friendly and helpful. (3) You're getting better at taking turns. (4) Your mum will be pleased. (5) Can you keep it up? . . . Well I think so.

Example	*Setting event*	*Behaviour*
3	Teacher asks group 1 to try and get 9/10 on their spelling check this week	Samina and James have 9 spellings correct

Praise statement

(1) Let's see . . . Samina and James, that's good. (2) You both got 9 out of 10 correct. (3) Third time for Samina and the first time for you, James. Well done. (4) Keep this up and you'll find spelling really easy. (5) Same again next week? . . . Well, have a try.

Partial praise statements

When a lesson is in full progress, shorter forms of praise are obviously more feasible. These should include the first two elements of a full praise statement: (1) gaining attention and showing approval, and (2) saying why you're pleased.

> *Example 1*: '(1) Well done, Class 4, (2). Everyone's working hard'.
> *Example 2*: 'Kay, good reading'.
> *Example 3*: 'Group Two, good listening'.

Praise must be used very often if it is to be effective in encouraging desired behaviours. It may not be easy to find the words or to deliver them naturally to begin with. Therefore, it is important to prepare yourself with praise statements which relate to your expectations and setting. It is helpful to practise them out loud before trying them out in class.

You might also practise reflecting on things you have achieved during the day and praising *yourself*. For instance 'I did alright with that art lesson . . . It was well-organised and the children produced some striking silhouettes.' For a *teacher* needs feedback and encouragement too — and you may be your own main source of praise at work!

Delivering praise

If praise is to mean something to pupils it must be said sincerely and in a way which is appropriate in the context of their relationship with their teacher.

Once again we would stress the importance of non-verbal communication. The first essential is to show approval not only in words but through eye contact and smiling. With younger children the praise message should be supported by warmth in the voice, and also perhaps by physical contact, such as ruffling the child's hair or patting his shoulder. However, a low-key approach is more appropriate with older pupils, more 'sophisticated' young children or those whom the teacher has not known long. In these circumstances bodily contact must definitely be avoided. If when you praise, children look embarrassed or start to snigger this is your cue to use a more 'deadpan' approach. Otherwise to them it may seem as if you are overdoing it — 'Joyce Grenfell style'.

A teacher's manner when praising will reflect not only his relationship with the children concerned, but also his personal style. If you are not a demonstrative person, don't act out of character. Praise must be delivered in ways which come most naturally and comfortably if it is to be sustained by teachers and believed by pupils.

This brings us to the point that praise should be sincere and truthful. It must be seen by both pupils and teacher to be matched to the achievement that earned it. To praise effusively when a child completes a routine task may not only feel forced and unjustified to the teacher, it may also lead his pupils to suspect insincerity, sarcasm — or worse! By clearly defining the behaviours you wish to see, and being willing to acknowledge the ordinary, you will make it easier to be truthful and sincere when reflecting their achievements back to the children.

121

Finally, praise must avoid any hint of criticism. Many teachers find this difficult, particularly when a child or group has recently misbehaved. Whether criticism is explicit or simply implied by a grudging or incredulous tone, it will neutralise the effect of the praise it accompanies. Praise is the thing of the moment. It is a consequence for appropriate behaviour and should be uncontaminated by events which took place at other times or in other places.

These general guidelines for delivering praise are summarised in Table 8.3.

Table 8.3: Delivering praise

Show approval (eye contact, facial expression, voice tone etc.)
Praise in a way that fits which children's ages, your relationship with them and your personal style
Match praise to the achievement that earned it
Be sincere and truthful
Avoid any hint of criticism

CHOOSING ADDITIONAL REWARDS

It is important to add to praise a selection of rewards of different types which may appeal to your pupils. A varied 'menu' of possible rewards is helpful for two reasons. First it can be useful to provide a range of rewards *as well as* praise for differing kinds and levels of achievement. Variety is of value in itself. Secondly, whilst we may hope that children will derive satisfaction from their work and be motivated by praise and feedback about progress, these may not be sufficient in all cases particularly with younger or less successful children. There may also be individual members of your class who are simply not interested in the rewards which generally appeal. For these children alternative rewards will be needed.

Let us now outline some of the considerations which need to be borne in mind when making the selection.

Choose rewards which are already known to be reinforcing

There are several ways to find out which rewards are already effective for a group of children. The most obvious is to simply observe the children. Note their reaction to praise; which activities and tasks they choose, ask for or seem to enjoy; how they spend free time. Notice too their choice of companions, the interests they speak of and the jobs they ask to do. All these observations will provide useful information as to *current* reinforcers. You could always ask children what they would like to happen when they have produced good work or behaved well in class. This may be in the form of open questions or by asking them to choose from a prepared list. It is important to include a selection from differing reward types — and to subject the items to a feasibility check. Where possible it is best to use those which are easy to deliver and are most general in their application across situations and with different children.

Vary your choice

A wide selection of rewards enables you to accommodate variations in children's interests across the group and over time. It also ensures that those you arrange hold their reward value, since you will be able to ring the changes.

Make sure children have experienced an event before using it as a reward

It is clearly important that children know what it is that they are working for. Therefore new activities or other events which you wish to introduce as reinforcers must be experienced by all initially. Once children have experienced an activity on 'free trial' and have enjoyed it, the activity can then be used as a reward. It can be removed from its place on the 'free trial' list and placed on the list of rewards to be given for desirable behaviour and achievements.

Choose only those rewards which you are free to offer or withhold

There will be occasions when children's behaviour does not warrant a particular reward and so it must be withheld or delayed. It is therefore essential to avoid using any event or item which it is *the child's right to have*. Included here are any activities which form a part of the child's curriculum. It may be fine to allow extra reading time as part of a free choice activity but it is certainly *not* permissible to use a pupil's access to individual reading sessions with the teacher as an activity reward. Similarly when using edible rewards, it is one

ie pudding etc.

123

thing to withhold a small sweet as a reward because a pupil has not behaved appropriately; it is quite another matter to make a child miss her pudding at lunchtime!

Make use of immediate rewards that can be exchanged

Praise is an immediate reward: it can be given as and when 'good' behaviour happens. Token rewards such as points are also useful as immediate rewards because they can be given for different behaviours and are relatively easy to deliver at the time they are earned. They can also be exchanged for a variety of activities and other rewards which can be set up at, perhaps, fixed times as convenient. However, we would emphasise that if the children will work for points *alone* then it is best to *use* points alone, only introducing further rewards if the additional reward value and variety they provide is necessary.

The ultimate test of your choice among rewards is that those you choose are in fact effective in strengthening the appropriate behaviour they follow. Your initial choice may need to be amended in the light of experience with your pupils in your particular circumstances. However, by keeping in mind the considerations we have outlined you increase your chances of success. They are summarised in Table 8.4.

Table 8.4: Choosing additional rewards

Choose rewards which are already reinforcing for your pupils
Vary your choice
Make sure the children experience an event before putting it on your list of rewards to be earned
Choose only those rewards you are free to offer or withhold
Make use of immediate rewards that can be exchanged

GETTING REWARDS TO WORK

Having identified and prepared rewards which are most likely to be suitable for your pupils and which are feasible in your situation, the question is how to make the most effective use of them over the days and weeks. Some guidelines for getting rewards to work are now introduced.

Accept and reward small steps towards the behaviour you want

There may be a number of social behaviours which children on entry to your class do not show at all or which are only partially correct. They may not yet have learned to work together in small groups or to accept one another's mistakes. They may not have met your classroom routines before nor be able to keep to new rules. In these circumstances we cannot expect children to present us with exactly the behaviour we want straight away. We must be prepared to accept steps towards the behaviour we want and work towards gradual improvement, perhaps through a series of teaching steps and opportunities to practise the new skills. For example, when we considered the teaching of new routines we outlined breaking these down into separate behaviours which constitute the chain. Thus we give separate instructions for each step in the sequence, and reward successful completion of each step before giving instructions for the next one in the sequence. Gradually we begin to amalgamate the separate parts of the routine to the point where the children complete the whole without extra instructions or prompts.

Alternatively we might accept successive approximations to the complex behaviour we want. To illustrate this process, imagine we wish to teach a child to play a musical instrument, a recorder. We may accept the production of any sound initially and reward this. Gradually as techniques are learned, we would raise the expectations, being more selective about the sounds which we reward. When used together with feedback on children's performance, we thus direct pupils' attention to the notes which were accurate and what they did which was correct. In this way we help them to make discriminations among the notes they produce and to begin their own 'quality control'. By giving them feedback pupils are directed to monitor their own behaviour and its effect on the sounds produced. This gradual *shaping* of behaviour, in which successive approximations to the ultimate desired behaviour are accepted and rewarded, is a natural process which is commonly used to teach social behaviours. It might be used to teach children classroom rules, courtesy behaviours, sharing and play skills. It is also an integral part of the step-by-step teaching of complex educational skills (see, for example, Vargas, 1977).

Always pair rewards with feedback

We would reiterate the importance of incorporating feedback whenever you reward children, be it for keeping to rules, being helpful or succeeding with their work. Remember that feedback lets the children know what they did that was appropriate and how they are improving. It helps them to establish connections between the circumstances of their behaviour and its natural outcomes. The association of feedback with rewarding events will enhance the value which this knowledge of results has for children. They will then be more likely to be motivated by the natural outcomes of the behaviour itself and by their own achievements on their tasks.

Make sure you 'catch them being good'

To be effective as consequences, rewards must be clearly linked to appropriate behaviour both through the feedback given and by their timing. 'Good' behaviour must be rewarded quickly, preferably as it happens. Hence the advantage of using your own attention and approval and, in some situations, token rewards. They are easy and quick to deliver.

Mistiming can lead to problems. If a teacher praises a child for working quietly but fails to notice that he has actually interrupted his work to listen to a friend, the child receives an ambiguous message. Thus his teacher's words refer to working but her timing associates praise with not working! Therefore, as far as possible without disrupting the lesson, it is important to give attention to appropriate behaviour as it happens. If you miss one opportunity to praise particular children, never mind — but make sure you seize the next. If there are special circumstances in which you feel praise is best deferred, make sure you do not delay too long and that your praise does not coincide with any unwanted behaviour by the children concerned.

Be persistent

A behaviour may be weak and infrequent, not because a child has not learned to act in this way, but because he has not learned where, or perhaps when, it is appropriate to behave in this way. Thus behaviours which are in themselves quite easy to perform, such as raising one's hand to ask or tell or walking in line, may be seen infrequently. The task for the teacher then is to teach the children to perform these behaviours as and when they are required: to strengthen a particular behaviour as a response to certain circumstances. The pattern in which rewards are given over a period of time is essential to this process of strengthening a behaviour when it occurs at the right place and the right time.

It is natural to notice and to be pleased on the first occasions that children show desirable behaviour and to react with praise and perhaps some other reward. However, when behaviours are not difficult to perform or when we expect them anyway, it is also natural to overlook these behaviours after their initial appearance and to subsequently fail to reward them. Yet it is necessary to be persistent. The teacher must keep on noticing and rewarding an appropriate behaviour until such time as it becomes a well-established response to its particular setting events. Otherwise the behaviour will remain weak and if it goes without reward may fade away altogether. Rewards must be given over a period of time for the connection between setting event, behaviour and consequence to be strengthened and the desired behaviour to become well-established in response to particular circumstances.

Be consistent and fair

It is important that the behaviour is rewarded consistently over time, for a child to learn to respond appropriately to particular setting events. If the desired behaviour is followed by teacher attention on one day but its opposite, unwanted behaviour, is reacted to by the teacher on the following day, the child (and her neighbours) will receive ambiguous information about which behaviour is desired. Their behaviour may become equally inconsistent! Furthermore their teacher may inadvertently strengthen unwanted behaviour if he reacts to this more often than to appropriate behaviour.

Similarly it is crucial that rewards are distributed evenly throughout the class group. If some pupils or groups are praised for sitting and working quietly and others are overlooked, confusion can again occur. Indeed a sense of unfairness can develop, particularly if those overlooked when seated quietly are told off for making noise or leaving their seat. So it is important to include children whom you may personally find less attractive and appealing!

By deciding in advance those behaviours which are to be

127

established it is easier to make sure that 'good' behaviour is rewarded, regardless of *who* behaves. In this way you ensure that rewards are given fairly and consistently amongst the children and over time.

Use more praise than corrections

The number of times praise is given must greatly exceed the number of corrections. This is the essence of a positive pattern of consequence management (see Chapter 2). We cannot hope to eliminate unwanted behaviour altogether but we can still maintain a positive *imbalance*. 'Concentrating on the positive' can be translated into making sure you keep a praise-to-corrections ratio of between 3:1 and up to 10:1 (see Medland and Vitale, 1984). Thus if four corrections are given during a lesson, the teacher should make at least twelve praise statements and preferably far more, say about 40. Even experienced teachers find this ratio is not easy to judge for oneself initially. So it may be helpful to begin by *counting* the number of times you reward and correct in a lesson (see Chapter 10) and practising until the ratio is at least 3:1. Then you might find it easier to judge when you have 'got the imbalance right', without having to count. This positive imbalance will help sustain a positive atmosphere in class and make it more likely that pupils will learn and maintain appropriate behaviour.

We would point out that this ratio of reward to corrections applies at the specific as well as the general level. For instance, if a teacher corrects a child or group for misbehaviour she returns to praise that individual or group at least two or three times before the end of the lesson. Preferably she would catch them showing appropriate behaviour which is incompatible with their previous misbehaviour (for example, sharing rather than snatching). However praise for any 'good' behaviour would fulfil the basic intentions here. These are to restore the positive imbalance to its level of at least 3:1 before the end of the lesson and to demonstrate that the teacher does give credit where it is due.

Praise often and evenly over time

The availability of additional rewards will depend on the achievement required to earn them and the arrangements which are necessary. For example, points might only be available to children when a piece of work is completed. Special activities or privileges may only be feasible at certain times of the day. However it is essential that *praise* is given very often indeed during the course of each lesson and day.

When working to establish a new or weak behaviour it is necessary to notice children behaving in this way and to praise this on as many occasions as possible. Later the frequency of praise can be reduced gradually as the behaviour becomes established. However it is important even then to keep rewarding on an occasional basis, for *intermittent reinforcement*, such as praising the group and individuals now and again for keeping long established rules, is very powerful in maintaining behaviour.

So a teacher may be concentrating on teaching certain new behaviours and giving praise very often for each. Alternatively she may be giving praise for a range of well-established behaviours, on an occasional basis for each. In either case she will need to share her praise evenly among all the members of her class and keep the ratio of praise to corrections high. Thus an average of one praise statement per minute would not be too great an estimate, but is not nearly so frequent as it might seem. Time yourself, you may be surprised!

Here we see the value of partial praise statements, they are brief and to the point. The cost effectiveness of praise can also be increased by naming several individuals in a single praise statement and, when justified, praising a group or the whole class as a single unit.

Further, incorporating feedback in praise statements helps children to eventually become more independent — seeing the outcomes of their appropriate behaviour for themselves and relying less on rewards their teacher gives them personally.

These guidelines for making effective use of rewards in class are summarised in Table 8.5.

Table 8.5: Getting rewards to work in class

Accept and reward small steps to the behaviour you want
Always pair rewards with feedback
Make sure you 'catch the children being good'
Be persistent
Be consistent and fair
Use more praise than corrections
Praise often and evenly over time

MAKING THE MOST OF REWARDS FROM OTHER SOURCES

When children are aware of and appreciate the natural outcomes of their behaviour, their 'good' behaviour becomes less dependent on rewards personally delivered by their teacher. Thus natural rewards from other sources free the teacher from a time-consuming responsibility. They also further the longer-term goals of a positive system of management. These are that children begin to take control of their own behaviour and that they generalise appropriate behaviour to other situations. We therefore conclude by considering some other sources of rewards. For in order to establish their value it is essential that they do in fact occur!

Educational outcomes

It is essential that natural rewards are provided through children's work in order to keep them behaving in ways which assist their progress.

Reaching curricular objectives

Design a curriculum that has approp. objectives for each child

We stress the value of organising the curriculum as a sequence of carefully selected objectives which are specified in terms of what the children must *do* in order to meet learning objectives. Then the children can see their progress as clearly as the teacher can. In attaining the objectives, they receive the natural consequences of their efforts. More finely graded steps towards these objectives can be arranged which provide more frequent measures of progress and success. Each of these steps can be as small as the teacher wishes so that even when children encounter difficulties their progress, though it may be slow, can be measured and visible even on a day-to-day basis (see Solity and Bull, 1987).

Using skills and information

It is vital that a teacher seeks ways in which the children can *use* from the outset the skills and information which they are learning in class. To take simple examples, a teacher encourages the children to use new French vocabulary and structures in communicating to each other, or to play 'tunes' written for the first notes they have learned to play on the recorder. Whether teaching them the format for letter writing or rapid addition of HTU, (hundreds, tens, units) the emphasis should be the same: let them use their skills as purposefully and meaningfully as possible.

If teaching objectives are to have relevance, it must be primarily in their usefulness now or in the future. Even when their usefulness is in laying foundations for learning future skills or, much later, passing exams it is essential to provide applications *now* rather than expect children to work for very long-term goals. Regular and frequent quizzes, exercises and tests — which might contribute to grades — can be valuable in sustaining children's attention for material which is not readily applicable *now* to real or near-real situations. The teacher will also need to make the most of record systems used within school or establish her own, based on a cumulative record of children's progress over the days and weeks of the year.

Varied activities

The pattern of activities across a session and the school day incorporates its own natural consequences. When more exciting and interesting activities follow more routine tasks, they provide natural rewards for completing the earlier tasks satisfactorily and on time.

Shared records of progress

Records of children's educational progress can highlight their improvements and bring them to their notice. Any type of record which helps the *children* see they are progressing can be used to provide feedback and encouragement. Group charts have their value. However, pupils whose progress is relatively slow will not be encouraged if they make comparisons with others. If their rate of progress through skills is reasonable, yet their attainment is still behind others, charts showing only the number of skills learned or pieces of work completed, without indicating *which* level of work it was, will provide a fairer indication. For they will relate to effort rather than to levels of educational attainment.

By building natural, positive consequences into the curriculum and the timetable, and assuring that they continue throughout the weeks, you will have many opportunities to link your own rewards to educational outcomes. In this way you facilitate the transfer of reinforcement away from yourself to the children's work itself.

131

Outcomes provided by other people

Not all appropriate behaviours have natural outcomes which are educational. Some behaviours are appropriate in that they contribute to the effective functioning of the social group, or the positive atmosphere of the classroom. Many of these centre on sharing: sharing materials, space and the teacher's time. They involve acknowledgement of others' rights, for example to privacy of space or belongings, or rights of access to equipment. These behaviours do facilitate effective learning in the group situation. However, many of them are naturally rewarded by *social consequences*: smiles, thanks and reciprocal actions of different kinds by other people.

Other children

By teaching appropriate social behaviours to all the children, using modelling, rules, prompts and rewards for 'good' behaviour, the teacher can enlist group members' assistance in rewarding each other, even when she is not at hand. Similarly, members of the whole group can share responsibility with their teacher for improving their behaviour in class. The 'group game' approach can be a useful starting point for this (see Chapter 9).

Colleagues

When looking for other people who can provide rewards, do not forget your colleagues and headteacher. The more sources with whom you can share delivery of rewards for good behaviour and performance the more broadly based the children's supply — and the more likely that they will continue to behave in these ways when you are not present and beyond their time in your class.

Parents

One of the most powerful alternative sources of rewards involving other people lies with parents. We would stress that when a teacher keeps parents informed of what he is doing and why, when he relates the positive aspects of children's behaviour and performance to their parents and invests time in enlisting their support and interest, he wins the most important allies of all. When these two sources of reward and encouragement (parents at home and teacher in school) are working together to encourage the same appropriate behaviours in class, the children receive consistent messages from both sources and are more likely to behave appropriately now and in the longer term.

In some schools communication with parents is limited to formal occasions: circulars, reports and parents' evenings. Yet there are also many examples of wider parent involvement: parent-assisted teaching in reading; community facilities in school; mother and toddler groups; parents helping in class. Communication may include regular and frequent discussions, weekly notes home to parents about good behaviour and progress made, daily home-school diaries, teachers freed to visit parents at home, and many other imaginative ideas besides. A positive system of management involves you in positive thinking: include the parents here and their support will pay dividends.

SUMMARY

In Chapter 8 we outlined in some detail the use of consequences to strengthen and maintain appropriate behaviour in class. We described ways in which you can prepare for your management of these consequences. We stressed the importance of effective praise and feedback and went on to discuss the selection of additional rewards. We offered guidelines on how to use rewards to greatest effect in promoting and maintaining 'good' behaviour. Finally we considered rewards from other sources that will help to maintain children's behaviour. These include the natural outcomes afforded by their work and by the behaviour of other people.

Meanwhile, what of unwanted behaviour? The system of positive management described is directed towards teaching, maintaining and generalising appropriate behaviour. However, unwanted behaviour will not be eliminated altogether and must therefore also be managed effectively. This is our focus in the next chapter.

9

Constructive Discipline

INTRODUCTION

The whole thrust of a positive system of management is directed towards eliciting and maintaining children's appropriate behaviour in class, and towards minimising the occurrence of unwanted behaviour. In an ideal world, the classroom environment may, perhaps, provide cues which elicited all the acceptable behaviours from the outset and the consequences would ensure they continued to be shown. However, this is not an ideal world and it would indeed be odd, even disturbing, if children behaved in the ways we wanted *all* the time!

Unwanted and undesirable behaviours in class are inevitable. Children may have learned some undesired behaviours as a result of their previous experiences in or out of school. They may not have yet learned the behaviours which are appropriate to their new class situation, and some may test out their teacher in order to establish what the new limits are. Many unwanted behaviours cannot simply be overlooked while the teacher waits for children to show appropriate behaviours. In this chapter therefore we outline some of the techniques available to the teacher in dealing with unwanted behaviours as they occur. Our emphasis is upon providing consequences which weaken and decrease these behaviours whilst retaining a constructive and positive atmosphere in class.

The effectiveness of the techniques relies upon the context for their use. As we pointed out in Chapter 2, a focus on negative behaviours can lead to the problem of the criticism trap, and the slippery slope to a negative pattern of management. Therefore the context for dealing with unwanted behaviours must always be one in which children's acceptable behaviours and steps towards them are being frequently noticed and rewarded. What follows is not presented as an alternative to all we have discussed previously but as a supplement to it. Always remember that the main objective is to minimise the risk of unwanted behaviours occurring: to teach the children appropriate behaviours and to elicit these instead. Within a positive system of management, a teacher's actions towards unwanted behaviours are far outweighed by the number of occasions she gives praise and other positive consequences. The intention is to weaken and decrease unwanted behaviour quickly and effectively, whilst simultaneously strengthening 'good' behaviour.

Unwanted behaviours can be a valuable source of information for the teacher. They can highlight ways in which his system of management may be improved. It is this issue, the teacher's perception of unwanted behaviour, that we consider first.

TAKING A GOOD LOOK AT UNWANTED BEHAVIOUR

What makes behaviour 'unwanted'?

Many teachers could list those behaviours which are inappropriate or undesirable in their particular setting. These may be things children do, or fail to do. A comparison of teachers' lists would highlight similarities but also show differences between their views of what constitutes 'unwanted' behaviour. These would depend on the particular classroom setting, the kinds of activities undertaken and the teacher's expectations of the children's behaviour according to their ages, previous experience and so on. We would also expect to find elements of personal preference within teachers' lists. We do not propose to list all possible misbehaviours here. However, we would point to four broad criteria which can lead to a behaviour being classified as 'unwanted'. There order is not intended to indicate a fixed priority.

The behaviour interrupts the child's own learning or that of his classmates: misbehaviour which interrupts a lesson.

The behaviour is antisocial in that it has detrimental effects on the child's interaction with his teacher or classmates, for example, taking another's belongings.

The behaviour may cause harm because it constitutes a risk to the child's safety or that of others, for example, swinging back on a chair, running in a busy corridor.

135

The behaviour results in loss or damage to school equipment or personal belongings, for example, breaking a school window, tearing the clothing of a classmate.

Some behaviours cause concern on more than one criterion. Some instances of fighting, for example, may be classified as unwanted on all four grounds.

Reasons for unwanted behaviour

We could often find a number of possible explanations or causes which can account wholly or in part for a child's misbehaviour including, perhaps, the contribution which may be made by factors within the child or within the family. A child's learning experiences outside school can be very pertinent in considering his behaviour. It is also recognised that certain types of medication can influence behaviour. Therefore it might sometimes help a teacher's understanding and interpretation of her pupil's behaviour if she has information about these various factors. Moreover, and especially when presented with uncharacteristic misbehaviours, there should be sufficient flexibility in a teacher's approach to ask the *child* what is wrong. He may just tell you! However, for practical purposes, to help decide what is to be done about behaviour in class, a teacher must look to the environment which she can effectively influence and control. Therefore we focus here on those influences upon misbehaviour which can be found within the classroom environment.

According to the behavioural model, a behaviour which is unacceptable can arise from problems at any point in the sequence 'setting events — behaviour — consequences'. The circumstances may cue unwanted behaviour or may fail to cue a change from one appropriate behaviour to another. In either case the result is behaviour which is unacceptable because it occurs at the wrong place or time.

There may be problems associated with the behaviour itself. A child may not have learned how to respond in the appropriate way. He may have been taught by previous experience to behave in a different way given the setting events in question. These factors often result in no response or a response which is different from the expected one.

The consequences of a misbehaviour may be maintaining or even increasing it because these consequences are pleasant or desirable from the child's point of view. In this case the desirable outcomes for the child of misbehaving outweigh those of behaving appropriately. At other times appropriate behaviour may not be displayed because it has been overlooked, and hence weakened, over a period of time.

Some possible influences on unwanted behaviour are illustrated by the examples in Table 9.1.

Table 9.1: Possible influences on unwanted behaviour in class

Example	Possible reasons
Despite being told to 'settle down', children are talking instead of getting on with their individual work	1. Is 'table' seating predisposing the children to talk? (*physical setting*) 2. Are their tasks too easy or, perhaps, too hard? (*educational setting events*) 3. Do they know they are to work quietly? (*social setting events — rules*) 4. Does their teacher leave the children to get on unless they are talking? (*consequences*)
Some children shout and interrupt others during a discussion session with the teacher	1. Does their teacher frequently shout and interrupt? (*social setting events — modelling*) 2. Does the teacher sometimes allow those who shout or interrupt to continue speaking? (*consequences*) 3. Do other children laugh at their remarks? (*consequences*) 4. Has the teacher established his leadership authority? (*social setting events*)
Children at one table are squabbling over crayons, throwing a rubber back and forth and frequently out of their seats	1. Are there sufficient materials at this table? (*physical setting*) 2. Have these children learned how to share? (*behaviour*) 3. Is their teacher preoccupied elsewhere in the room? (*social setting events*)

Learning from children's unwanted behaviour

When a teacher constantly monitors pupils' behaviour she not only notices acceptable behaviour but can pick up signals from the children which tell her when all is not well. These enable her to be responsive to pupils' needs. For example, she may change the context by amending plans for part of the session when it is noted that pupils' attention is waning. More serious misbehaviours usually arise from small misdemeanours. By taking action before those warning signs develop further the teacher can avert potentially greater difficulties.

Misbehaviours not only assist the teacher to make corrections to the course of events at the time, but have implications for future planning. By taking note of recurrent unwanted behaviours, their context *and* the consequences which follow them, the teacher can estimate where the problem lies. She should then consider what changes to her arrangement of the classroom and its events she can make in order to improve the likelihood that children will behave in the desired ways in future.

Meanwhile, how does she *deal* with unwanted behaviours? As we shall see the teacher's responses may not be in the form of direct action on the unwanted behaviour. In fact they do not necessarily involve any interaction at all with the children concerned!

RESPONDING TO UNWANTED BEHAVIOURS

These behaviours may be presented by one individual or by different children on different occasions. They may involve more than one individual at one time. They may be active, such as a child leaving his seat, or passive, such as gazing out of the window. They may be appropriate at other times or in other situations but inappropriate here and now. Or they may be such that they would be wholly unacceptable in most circumstances. How a teacher responds to unwanted behaviours will be determined in part by how serious the effects of the behaviour are, or may be, to learning, social relations or safety. His response is largely determined by his interpretation of the behaviour in its particular context.

We shall now consider a range of options that are open to the teacher (Table 9.2) and that have the following advantages in common.

Table 9.2: Ways of dealing with unwanted behaviour

Ignoring the unwanted behaviour
    (rewarding appropriate behaviour instead)

Changing the context
    (1) changing the activity
    (2) providing help
    (3) changing the organisation
    (4) removing distractions
    (5) allowing the child to change context
    (6) using humour

Light techniques of control
    (1) signs and signals
    (2) moving in
    (3) calling them back to task
    (4) reminders about rules and routines
    (5) reminders about consequences

Using peer group influence
    (the group game)

Making the most of natural consequences

Stronger measures
    (1) the warning procedure
    (2) response cost
    (3) reparation
    (4) time out
    (5) removal to another room

(1) They help a teacher to stay calm in circumstances which are potentially distracting or difficult.

(2) They minimise the time spent in dealing with unwanted behaviours.

(3) They do not involve shouting, 'shaming' or corporal punishment, all of which are detrimental to the relationship between teacher and pupils.

The procedures we describe are *all* 'corrections'. They are ways of providing consequences which weaken and reduce unwanted behaviours. To be effective with individuals and the class as a whole, corrections must always be outnumbered by praise and other positive consequences in a ratio of at least 1:3. This is a point we stress even when considering the first option which, as you will see, does not involve responding to the unwanted behaviour at all.

Ignoring the behaviour

The teacher registers a child's unwanted behaviour but takes a conscious decision to ignore rather than respond to it directly. Within the behavioural model this procedure is known as *extinction*.

Extinction is the term used to describe the way a change in consequences can, over a period of time, weaken a behaviour. Essentially, outcomes which a child finds desirable are withheld so they no longer follow the behaviour they maintained. Extinction is most appropriate when teacher attention has inadvertently maintained a particular unwanted behaviour. This can happen even when the attention given is negative, as when a child persistently calls out and receives teacher attention in the form 'Robert, stop calling out!'

There are one or two problems associated with extinction. First, it invariably results in a temporary spate of the unwanted behaviour before it finally peters out. Therefore the behaviours you choose to treat in this way must be those which *can* be ignored, which do not stop the lesson or cause harm to the child or others. Secondly, it may seem odd and even ineffectual to notice an unwanted behaviour and yet *do* nothing.

However the effectiveness of extinction is increased when it is coupled with giving attention to the alternative, desired, behaviour. So instead of doing nothing when an unwanted behaviour is noticed, the teacher uses it as her cue to praise children who are behaving appropriately. This will often succeed in reminding the 'target' child as to what he should be doing and lead him to behave appropriately. After a short time the teacher can then praise him for behaving as he should, and would praise him several more times during the rest of the lesson. This coupling of ignoring and reward can be used with individuals or the whole group, as the following examples illustrate.

Example one

A class rule is to work hard and finish work set. Lisa is daydreaming, gazing at her fingernails. Her teacher praises another child at Lisa's table: 'Good, Simon, you're working hard, and soon you'll have finished'. Lisa continues to dream. Her teacher praises someone else, 'Carol, that's neat, keep up the hard work'. Lisa starts working. After a short pause her teacher praises her, 'Good, Lisa, you're working hard'. During the rest of the lesson the teacher finds three or four more opportunities to praise Lisa.

Example two

In Mrs James' class, the rule is to put up your hand to ask or tell. The children keep this rule fairly well, except during 'news' sessions, when they call out and interrupt one another. Mrs James realises that she has, in fact, sometimes allowed children to carry on speaking when they have called out. So she decides that she will no longer attend to children when they call out but only when they quietly put up their hands. As a way of dealing with the expected spate of calling out, Mrs James plans to use calling out as her cue to attend to those who are quiet and have their hands up. She will say something like, 'Good, Timmy, Jane, Clare . . . you have your hands up'. She will ask one of these children to speak by adding, 'What do you want to tell us?'. At first children continue to call out in news sessions and even for a while call louder and more often. Mrs James sticks to her plan, ignoring calls and praising children when they sit quietly with their hand up even though they must take turns to speak. She mentions different children on different occasions so that her praise is fairly shared around the class. She is careful to 'catch' and praise persistent offenders when they *do* put up their hand. In this way calling out always goes without reinforcement; whereas putting up a hand is followed, as often as possible, by Mrs James' attention and praise. Eventually calling out becomes a very rare occurrence in news sessions and Mrs James can gradually reduce the attention she pays to children quietly putting up their hand.

Once established this behaviour will be maintained by the less frequent reward of being asked to speak, providing these requests are shared fairly among the group and Mrs James is not tempted to attend to occasional calling out.

Note that in the above examples the children who showed unwanted behaviour were not ignored altogether! Only their unwanted behaviour was ignored; they received praise when behaving appropriately. Note also that the teachers were free to make *some* response. It was not directed towards the 'target' children or their unwanted behaviours but served to highlight the behaviour the teachers wanted to see.

To be effective then, the pattern of ignoring and reward should be kept up over a period of time. So a teacher must be prepared to keep on ignoring the unwanted behaviour *whoever* is behaving in this way. To attend to the unwanted behaviour occasionally will serve to maintain it very effectively!

- The extinction procedure is useful when:

(1) The behaviour is not serious in its effects.
(2) It would interrupt the smooth running of the lesson to attend to it.
(3) The behaviour is not reinforced by classmates, otherwise their behaviour would continue to maintain it.
(4) The procedure is coupled with teaching an appropriate alternative behaviour. This must include returning to 'target' children to reward appropriate behaviour several times during the lesson.

This option is particularly appropriate if the behaviour has previously been maintained by teacher attention.

Changing the context

This group of responses again involves little or no action directly on the unwanted behaviour. Rather the teacher interprets the context for the behaviour and seeks to change those elements of the context which are promoting it.

Changing the activity

We have already referred to this response if a lesson is not working out as well as was hoped, and pupils' interest is waning. It may involve changing the tasks in which some of the children are involved, or changing the pace of the session, or inserting an attention-gaining activity, such as a quiz. Being prepared to change course is essential and demands not only the willingness to alter plans or adopt contingency plans but also, sometimes, quick 'thinking on one's feet'!

Providing help

An individual's off-task behaviour may be interpreted as being related to difficulties with his task or the instructions he received. His teacher will not wish to give much attention to his off-task behaviour. However, she may quickly redirect him to the task and then check to see if help is needed, providing it for him when necessary.

Changing the organisation

This may be the teacher's response to some off-task behaviours. It may be simply that materials can be redistributed or better positioned so as to avoid recurrence of unwanted squabbles, waiting time and so on. In some cases, the most effective response may be to change seating position or groupings, for example to make more room.

Removing distractions

This can often be achieved without interrupting the lesson and is often preferable to moving the children themselves. Curtains can be drawn on events going on outside or curious objects temporarily removed from display when these are interpreted by the teacher as causing distractions.

Allowing the child to change context

This is a useful way of 'defusing' the situation for an individual. It involves permitting the child who is in some way distressed to go to another place until such time as they feel composed and ready to begin work again. It can be a useful response to certain behaviours, for example, hiccups and fits of the giggles. There is no negative element in providing such a change of context; it is merely a chance for the child to recover herself and begin again when composed. This option must, of course, be used cautiously. There must be a suitable 'other place' to go. There must be trust that the child will respond appropriately if she goes out of sight — and will return! This is not a technique to be used liberally therefore, but is useful in specific situations.

Using humour

Unlike most of the other techniques included here the use of humour does not change the context for children in any direct way. However, we include it within this group for it can serve to change the social context of a situation. Humour is not a technique which can be brought into play just as or when needed. However, if the teacher is able to see the funny side of a situation he can sometimes save the day with a humorous remark where other approaches would have failed.

Jokes and humorous remarks perform many functions in the communication between teacher and pupils (Walker and Adelman, 1976) and they can be effective in relieving a tense situation. This is probably because they involve a sudden shift of meaning which causes everyone to see the situation in a different way: that is, changing the context.

143

Teacher responses which seek to change the context must do so with minimal interruption to learning. They are most appropriate when the factors within the physical, educational and social contexts which are eliciting the unwanted behaviour are accurately identified and easily altered.

Using light techniques of control

The immediate intentions of these teacher responses are to interrupt the unwanted behaviour and direct the child to the desired behaviour. In some cases, light techniques also involve pointing out the links between behaviour and consequences or between setting events and behaviour. However, whilst these are responses to unwanted behaviour, it is to the alternative *desired* behaviour to which the teacher's words will refer.

Signs and signals

These are commonly and effectively used by teachers to interrupt unwanted behaviours from a distance with minimal interruption to the lesson. For example, if a group's discussion is becoming too loud and distracting others, the teacher may simply catch one member's eye and signal the instruction for reduced noise by gesture. Of course the signals used must be clear and should indicate what children should *do*, rather than merely signal disapproval by, for example, frowning.

Moving in

When seating position or the nature of the lesson prevents the teacher catching the child's eye, light physical intervention may be appropriate. For example, one might lightly touch a child's shoulder and point to his book to bring him out of his reverie or quietly remove the object a child is playing with during a story. The intention is to interrupt the child's undesired behaviour and prompt him to behave appropriately, without other children being distracted.

In this type of direct intervention the teacher is using his higher status rights: to invade personal space and to even touch the child or his belongings. However, whilst higher status can be used effectively in this way, proximity, touching belongings and, most important, touching the child must be used with caution. First, overuse of these techniques can signal disrespect for the other person. Secondly, if used with the wrong child or in the wrong manner a major confrontation can result. The teacher has higher status rights only in so far as his pupils acknowledge them. With older pupils the overuse or misuse of these rights can lead to a challenge of the teacher's authority. The golden rule of any such techniques, and particularly touching, is that they should *never* be used in anger but in a calm, matter of fact manner. Indeed in some cases, particularly with older pupils, touching may not be acceptable at all.

Calling them back to task

Speaking to the children concerned is perhaps the most common teacher response to misbehaviour and might range from a 'quiet word' close to the 'target' child to a remark made across the room. The most important features of verbal interventions are that they must be brief and must be *task-related*. A lengthy tirade listing all the unwanted behaviours presented by the child since last Thursday will do nothing for the smooth running of the lesson, the child's willingness to behave in future, or the teacher's leadership authority!

Verbal interventions may simply take the form of a question related to the child's task, making no reference to the unwanted behaviour. A teacher might merely remind the group (not calling attention to the individual) of the time remaining to complete their tasks. Many variations are possible and if they do not draw attention to the unwanted behaviour, nor to the child who presented it, all the better.

Dealing with the child and the unwanted behaviour directly must be approached with caution. When you do approach individuals directly, make sure it is only occasionally and always refer to the behaviour which you *want* to see, for example, 'Joe, let's see you working quietly'; 'Helen, let Roger have a turn'.

Reminders about rules and routines

A teacher may interrupt an unwanted behaviour with a signal to the individual or group concerned and remind pupils of the setting events pertinent at the time. It may be a class rule, an instruction relating to their learning activity or, as in the following example, a routine.

Red group have completed their paintings and are milling about their table pointing to each other's pictures with sticky hands. Their teacher quickly calls red group to the sink and checks their understanding of the clear-up routine starting with, 'What do you do as soon as you have finished your painting?'. She then keeps

145

an eye on them as they perform the routine and gives praise either as they complete each step or when they have finished.

Such reminders do give a child or group the benefit of the doubt in that they may have forgotten or misunderstood what is required. The teacher uses the unwanted behaviour as a cue for her to underline the circumstances which prevail and the corresponding appropriate behaviour. Where it is felt that individuals or groups are indeed unsure of what to do, then regular reminders and rehearsals of rules and routines should be provided at other times, such as the beginning of lessons.

Reminders about consequences

The intention here is to help the child make the link for herself between behaviour and outcomes so that she can begin to regulate her own behaviour. For example, a teacher catches a child's attention when she is retying her ribbon (again!) and points out that the child will have time to do her free choice activity if her work is finished in five minutes. Note that again the teacher confines himself to the *desired* behaviour (finishing work) and the consequences of finishing on time.

Light techniques of control are effective when:

(1) They draw attention to the desired behaviour (and perhaps its setting events or consequences) rather than to the unwanted behaviour.

(2) They cause minimal interruption to the learning of individuals and group.

(3) The amount of teacher attention involved is minimal.

(4) They are given in a relaxed and matter-of-fact manner so that they are consistent with leadership status and good modelling.

(5) The teacher uses praise statements once 'target' children have behaved appropriately for a short time, and keeps a praise-to-corrections ratio of at least 3:1.

Light techniques of control assume that the teacher has the general cooperation of the group and that teacher and pupils are working together in the same direction, with a common goal.

Concentrate on desired behaviour than undesired when using light technique methods of control.

Using peer group influence

The teacher is not the sole source of social reinforcement in the classroom. Other children, particularly close friends, are a powerful source of positive reinforcement in the classroom as well as in the playground. Difficulties arise when behaviours which the teacher would not reinforce are rewarded by other pupils. An effective way to ensure that classmates and teacher are reinforcing similar behaviours is to provide rewards for the group *as a whole* when the behaviour of all the children meets the teacher's requirements. Group-centred reinforcement is a way of enlisting the assistance of the group in supporting the classroom situation most conducive to learning. Using peer-group influence, the teacher shares responsibility for classroom management with his pupils.

A variety of studies report the success of the so-called 'game approach' to group-oriented management (see, for example, Merrett and Wheldall, 1978). These involve children earning points or other tokens of some kind for good behaviours, as if it were a game. The 'game' may be organised on a competitive basis, teams with the most good behaviour points earning certain privileges. It may be one in which everyone can win provided the group earns sufficient good behaviour points. As you will see from the case study which follows, the game approach centres on the use of consequences for *appropriate* behaviour. Some teachers may use this approach as part of their usual management of 'good' behaviour. However, we feel it is likely to have value as a shorter-term measure for managing *unwanted* behaviours which are wide-spread within the group.

Example

Mr Wright found his new group of second-year juniors boisterous and giggly. The children had been together for a year and knew each other well. It was a cohesive group and some class 'clowns' were also well established. Mr Wright experienced difficulty in overcoming the group's consequences merely by praising children when they were working and ignoring them when they were not. Difficulties were most apparent during morning sessions, when activities usually involved individual work on Maths and English tasks. He therefore decided to arrange a reward for the whole group based on everyone's behaviour during the morning. Having checked that the children were working on suitable tasks and that seating was as conducive to individual tasks as room and furniture allowed, he wrote his three basic ground rules for a wall poster:

(1) We stay in our seats.
(2) We work quietly.
(3) We put up our hands to ask or to tell.

Mr Wright then explained to the pupils what would happen. He drew their attention to the three rules and told them that he would make checks from time to time during morning sessions to see if everyone was keeping the rules. When he found they were, he would put one point on the board. If sufficient points were earned during the morning, the last 15 minutes of the session would be free choice activities. Mr Wright prepared a selection of favourite activities and games which could be offered at the end of the morning. He set the number of checks at 20 and set the initial target which would earn the group reward at 15. Thus he had provided for frequent checks initially and for correspondingly frequent feedback to the children about how well they were doing. He felt his initial target (15) gave the group a chance to succeed, even though they might miss some points. At the start of the session he reminded the children of the rules, and the target score they must earn to have 15 minutes end-of-morning free choice activities.

The system gave Mr Wright certain advantages. He frequently scanned the room anyway and so children would not anticipate when they were being checked for scoring purposes. He could check as often as was convenient for him and, if he wished, could vary the target as the group improved. He could also distribute his checks across the morning as he wished, so that he could, if he desired, make the final check just 15 minutes before the end of the lesson. He could also vary the free choice activities offered as interests changed and could follow up some suggestions made by the children.

Each time he made an 'official' check Mr Wright gave the children feedback, praise and a point if all were keeping the rules. He also told them when a check had not earned them a point. He continued encouragement and reward for individual work as he had previously. He was pleased to find that adding a group reward to his own reinforcement for individual work had the desired effect. Children worked more quietly, more work was completed in the shorter session and, in the absence of a response from their audience, witty remarks by class 'clowns' were heard less often during work time! Over time Mr Wright found that he needed to make 'official' checks of the group's behaviour less often and could reduce the corresponding target score which would earn fun activities.

Therefore as the appropriate behaviours became well established he needed to spend less time and effort on this aspect of management.

There are many possible variations on the game theme in class and further details about the practical application of the approach are described elsewhere (see, for example, Wheldall and Merrett, 1984b; Frankland, Pitchford and Pitchford, 1985). Some are more elaborate than others, employing a random timer to signal a check. They employ different kinds of token reinforcers: points, stars, even beads. They can also be used to improve many differing unwanted behaviours: failure to tidy away toys or materials; failure to move quietly and quickly from one part of school to another; slowness in starting work, etc. They are useful when an unwanted behaviour is shown by many children rather than one or two individuals.

An important corollary to the game approach — as to other techniques — is to point out to the children the advantages of the *natural* consequences when everyone keeps to the rules. These may be improved comfort and convenience for everyone or improved work performance. In Mr Wright's case there was the added advantage that when everyone worked hard there was some time for relaxation and fun after work. When the teacher points out these benefits to children from the start it is easier to withdraw the game gradually once 'good' behaviours are established. The natural consequences of behaving appropriately are then more likely to sustain the behaviours once the game approach is phased out.

Making the most of natural consequences

When children are working within a positive management system they automatically earn positive consequences for completing work satisfactorily and in the time available. Failure to do so carries costs: the opportunity to change activity may be delayed, social rewards temporarily withheld and so on. This use of the system itself and the natural costs which follow a failure to meet minimal requirements set by the teacher emphasises the children's own responsibilities.

When the teacher has set up the environment so that his pupils have every opportunity to succeed in meeting requirements and can receive positive outcomes for complying, he can afford to expect pupils to take their share of responsibility by trying their best to meet the requirements. The consequences for their behaviour are then determined more by children's behaviour within the system, rather than by any direct action by their teacher. His role in responding to

149

unwanted behaviour becomes more of an arbiter within the system than an enforcer of personal standards.

Major considerations here are that expectations of the children's behaviour and work are, in fact, realistic and the system is fair. These are, of course, the teacher's responsibilities!

STRONGER MEASURES

Now we move on to consider more persistent misbehaviours and those which have more serious effects. Behaviours which can seriously interrupt a child's own learning or that of his classmates, which can adversely affect social relationships within the group or, worse, can cause harm to anyone, require specific responses. First, these behaviours must be interrupted effectively. Secondly, the consequences which follow them must reduce their frequency quickly. We cannot afford to let children keep on repeating these misbehaviours. They must learn to control them quickly and, equally quickly, learn more appropriate alternative behaviour.

The phrase 'stronger measures' may initially bring to mind consequences for misbehaviour which are so unpleasant from a child's point of view that they would quickly deter him from repeating the misbehaviour. Severe reprimands, shaming, detention after school, referral to senior staff for a 'dressing down' or even smacking, may be called to mind. These are all forms of *punishment*: a term which, within the behavioural model, refers *specifically* to imposing unpleasant events for misbehaviour.

However, the use of unpleasant events with pupils in this way is very often disquieting for teachers. This is particularly the case when they realise that, to be effective in decreasing behaviour, punishment must be immediate and strong and must consistently follow the misbehaviour whenever it occurs. Moreover the use of punishment carries a number of negative side-effects for children and teachers which we would highlight at this point.

First, what a teacher sees as an unpleasant event the child may not, particularly if the 'punishment' involves individual or extensive adult attention (in public or in private). Many teachers expect that a severe 'telling-off' will decrease the misbehaviour it follows. The assumption here is that most children dislike being reprimanded. However, this may not always be the case. Most teachers have had children in their class whom they would describe as 'attention-seeking'. For these children *any* kind of teacher attention would be a desirable consequence for their behaviour. Thus even a severe reprimand is in danger of acting like a reinforcer, because it is one way of giving attention. This is another example of the 'criticism trap' (Becker, Engelmann and Thomas, 1975), discussed in Chapter 2.

To be effective, punishment must be consistent and follow the behaviour each time it occurs. It is easily negated in class by other consequences which may not be within the teacher's control at all times and which are likely to continue to reinforce and strengthen the behaviour. For example, the child gets his own way by hitting other pupils when the teacher is not present or is not looking.

Punishments carry their own repercussions. The more severe the punishment the more likely that the child will come to dislike the person who punishes and cooperation will therefore be lost. The child may seek ways to avoid punishment. He may learn to avoid extra homework or detention. He may even avoid the lesson by simply not turning up at the stated time. He may refuse to accept the punishment, further challenging his teacher's authority.

Finally, we would mention the risk that a teacher imposing punishment is providing an example of what, if seen from children, would be an unwanted behaviour. If she shouts, uses sarcasm or, at worst uses corporal punishment, she risks pupils being more likely to show undesirable behaviours towards classmates.

The 'stronger measures' we shall now describe are effective in decreasing unwanted behaviour but have fewer negative side-effects than punishment. They are therefore more suitable for use within a positive system of management. First we describe a *warning procedure* and then a group of measures which we term *sanctions*.

The warning procedure

Ignoring and rewarding or light techniques may have been tried for a period but the child's unwanted behaviour has persisted, or the behaviour may seriously interrupt teaching and learning. In these cases the warning procedure may be effective without recourse to other stronger measures. However, if the unwanted behaviour causes or is likely to cause harm, other action should be taken immediately, without giving a warning. In such cases the teacher does not have time to wait and see if the warning has the desired result!

Just as the effectiveness of praise is dependent on *what* is said and *how* it is said, so too with a warning. The warning procedure is outlined in Table 9.3.

Table 9.3: The warning procedure

(1) Gain attention and show that this is a warning
(2) Specify the *appropriate* behaviour
(3) Specify the consequence of non-compliance
(4) Keep the warning brief
(5) Return quickly to teaching and praising other children
(6) Praise the 'target' child once he is behaving appropriately (keep the 3:1 ratio)
(7) Only give the child one warning

Gain the child's attention and make it clear that this is a warning

The teacher can say, for example 'Stephen! This is a warning.' Remember the importance of voice tone, eye contact, facial expression and body posture here. They must all be consistent with the firm, even sharp, verbal message. If possible, it is better to be reasonably close to the child and a little aside from the main group than to deliver warnings across a crowded room. Shouting only conveys a loss of control. It can put a teacher's authority in doubt and may tempt the child to shout back. So the extent of your personal feelings must be kept to yourself.

Specify the appropriate behaviour

Again it is the appropriate, rather than the unwanted, behaviour that is drawn to the child's attention, for example, 'The rule is to let your friends do their work'.

Specify the consequence of non-compliance

Here the teacher states clearly what the child should do and what the consequence of non-compliance will be, for example, 'Keep the rule or I will separate you from your friends'. Different sanctions may be appropriate but it is essential that a teacher only gives warnings she is able and prepared to carry out.

Keep the warning brief

There is a risk otherwise of interrupting the lesson further and reinforcing the misbehaviour by prolonged teacher attention. It is important to avoid arguments at this point. An example of a full warning might be: '(1) Rachel! (2) The rule is to work hard and finish your work. Keep the rule (3) or you will have to finish work during free choice time'.

Return immediately to teaching and giving praise to other children

Contact with other pupils should be interrupted for no longer than is absolutely necessary. By returning to the rest of the group with praise statements and his usual manner, the teacher will help retain a positive atmosphere.

Give praise once the child behaves appropriately

Once the child has behaved appropriately for a short time, her teacher praises her appropriate behaviour and finds at least two further opportunities to praise the child during the lesson.

Only give the child one warning

Should the unwanted behaviour persist after one warning, the teacher follows through with the consequence stated. This may be one of a number of sanctions that we shall now describe.

Sanctions

These measures centre on removing pleasant events (rather than imposing unpleasant events), but we also include the child making up in some way for what he has done.

Sanction procedures are brought into effect *either*: when the misbehaviour stops teaching and learning, and has not responded to other corrections including the warning procedure; *or*: when the misbehaviour is so serious that it is likely to cause harm, that is, it must be stopped immediately and decreased very rapidly.

Response cost

This is the *removal of a pleasant event* as a consequence of misbehaviour. The misbehaviour carries 'costs' such as the loss of a privilege, free time, a favoured activity or perhaps points.

There are several important considerations when using response cost. First, the pleasant event which is removed must be one which a teacher is *free* to withdraw. Curricular activities and those to which the child has a right cannot be used in this way. Secondly, the privilege or event which is lost must be one that the child has experienced and does indeed find pleasant. She may not mind missing extra reading time or may prefer staying behind with her teacher to going out into the cold playground!

Thirdly, the 'cost' should be implemented without delay. To withdraw a privilege which would be available much later in the day would sever the connection between the misbehaviour and its consequences and would appear unfair. Delay in implementing response cost also risks the child avoiding the sanction and the teacher forgetting about it. Finally the 'cost' must be specific and shortlived, otherwise the incentive to start behaving appropriately is much reduced. Thus to sit and work apart from friends until a child has finished his piece of work might be appropriate, but to work in isolation for the whole day or, worse, every morning for a week would be inappropriate and would be likely to cause confusion and resentment.

Response cost, then, is to be used with caution and the 'cost' should be chosen with care. It is most effective when the teacher is using a wide range of rewards which are conditional on children's acceptable behaviour and can be withdrawn (see Chapter 8). It is appropriate to misbehaviours which interrupt learning rather than to those which are potentially harmful.

Reparation

This involves the child making up in some way for what he has done. Examples include cleaning up the mess he has made, helping to mend or pay for what is broken and helping the child he has hurt. Given the circumstances in which this procedure is likely to be implemented (that is, the behaviour has already caused harm) it is not normally preceded by a warning. However it may follow a period of 'time out', for example, after a tantrum. Whilst some supervision is often needed, it is important to avoid giving too much individual attention.

Time out (separation)

This involves *removing the child* from a situation which, for her, is reinforcing. The procedure assumes that a positive management system prevails, and that current classroom events are indeed pleasant from the point of view of the 'target' child. Then it is, for her, undesirable to be removed from these even for a *brief* period of 2–3 minutes.

Time out is intended to be dull. It should be spent in a quiet place which is distanced from the teacher and other children. It is not a good idea to actually remove a child from the classroom. A corridor does not meet the requirements of time out as it can be a most interesting and rewarding place! Furthermore, it is difficult to supervise a child who is outside the room and so further misbehaviours are more likely. It is therefore preferable to have a small part of the classroom and a certain chair which is deemed the 'separation' or 'time-out' area.

Once the child is separated from the rest of the class it is important that she does not engage in any potentially rewarding activity, such as playing, talking or working. Other children need to be prepared beforehand so that they ignore the child on 'time out' and continue with their own activities. Their teacher too should return immediately to teaching and encouraging the rest of the group. This is not a time to lecture the 'target' child but rather to continue the interesting events on which she is missing out.

It is the *removal* from reinforcement which is important, rather than the amount of time spent 'out'. Therefore after 2–3 minutes the teacher asks the child if she is ready to come back and to keep the rules. If 'Yes', then she may rejoin the activity and the incident is treated as closed. Her teacher makes sure he starts to use praise with her after she has behaved appropriately for a short time. Should the child not indicate that she is ready to return and keep the rules, she remains in the time out area for a further 2–3 minutes. She will then be asked again if she is ready to return and keep the rules.

Time out is useful only when used in the context of a positive classroom environment. It can be implemented immediately and during virtually any activity. Its effectiveness depends on the teacher's handling of the situation and his success in preparing other children to continue their activities and ignore the child who is separated.

Removal to another room

This is an extension of 'time out', and involves sending a child out of class to another room, which may be the office or other quiet place where the child would be supervised.

Should a child continue to misbehave after a short interval in the separation area, he is warned that if he does not sit quietly he will be sent to the office (or other designated room). If the misbehaviour continues, then after a short time the child should be sent to the other room, where 'time out' procedures will be conducted by another adult (see above).

Removal of this kind obviously involves other adults as well as the teacher. Therefore the procedures, including how the child will be dealt with in the office, need to be agreed by all those who may be involved. Supervision of the child must be guaranteed but should not involve lecturing, counselling or sympathetic attention. This sanction may carry a number of practical difficulties, for example, ensuring that the child reaches the other room and that his management is consistent. It would most probably be reserved for very difficult or intractible behaviours which are considered by all concerned to be sufficiently serious, harmful or persistent as to warrant removal from class.

Implementing sanctions

The steps involved in giving a sanction are similar to those involved in the warning procedure. However, now the *misbehaviour* and *its* probable consequences are specified. Just as with a warning, the teacher's words and manner should be firm and leave the child in no doubt as to the type of consequence which is to follow. The steps in implementing a sanction are shown in Table 9.4.

Table 9.4: Steps in implementing a sanction

Step 1 Gain attention
Step 2 Say what the unwanted behaviour is
Step 3 Say why the behaviour is unacceptable
Step 4 State the sanction warranted by this behaviour
Step 5 Give the instruction which implements the sanction

These steps are indicated in the following examples:

Example 1 '(1) Jason! (2) Throwing things (3) can hurt people and cause damage, and (4) puts you on 'time out' . . . (5) Sit there for a few minutes and think about what you *should* have been doing.'

Example 2 (After a warning). '(1) Julia! (2) You are making so much noise (3) that people can't hear me, and (4) I'll have to separate you from the class . . . (5) Sit over there for 2 minutes and be quiet'.

Once again, the teacher would return his attention to the group as soon as possible, and would include the 'target' child in his praise once she had complied with the sanction *and* started to behave appropriately.

You may have some reservations about whether children will comply with sanctions. The first point here is that, like all aspects of classroom management, stronger measures need to be planned and prepared. When a teacher is sure of what action to take, and why, she is more likely to feel unruffled and in control of events. This will be communicated to the child through her calm and firm manner. The child will then be more likely to acknowledge her authority with compliance. The paradox of leadership applies here. If, as you implement a sanction, you allow yourself to doubt that the child will comply, he is *less* likely to do so. Expect that he will comply, and he most probably will!

Secondly, stronger measures are used in the context of a positive system of management in which children are encouraged to behave appropriately and are rewarded for doing so. Very many of the appropriate behaviours for which they receive praise involve following teacher instructions. Corrections occur less often and warnings and sanctions are relatively unusual. Thus the context alone is likely to facilitate children's compliance with the instructions given in warnings and sanctions.

Stronger measures are intended to be used constructively rather than punitively. They are used to safeguard the learning, relationships and safety of individuals and the class as a whole. Furthermore they are for use *only* when other measures have been unsuccessful or the misbehaviour is so serious in its effects that immediate strong measures are necessary. Therefore these measures should not be viewed as a teacher's 'secret armoury'. They can be fully explained to the class in advance of their use. The children will then know what to expect and will understand more fully the reasons for warnings and sanctions. Being open with the class will help to enlist the group's cooperation and the 'target' child's compliance in the event that these stronger measures are indeed brought into effect.

General guidelines for using stronger measures

Whilst the measures we have described carry fewer risks than punishment, we would advocate their use within the following conditions.

The teacher is clear about which misbehaviours warrant stronger measures

Consider the misbehaviours which would stop teaching and learning in different lessons. Some misbehaviours may have this effect in most lessons; others may apply only when certain types of equipment or presentation are used. For all these misbehaviours, other techniques and the warning procedure should be tried before using sanctions.

157

Which behaviours would be anticipated to cause harm to the child himself or to others? Which would be likely to cause harm or damage when using apparatus or equipment? These are behaviours which must be stopped immediately with an appropriate sanction.

Linking specific measures to certain types of misbehaviour will assist the teacher to use them fairly and consistently. Moreover, once she is clear about her choice and intended use of warnings and sanctions she is in a position to explain them to pupils. It is important to stress to children the reasons which underlie these measures and to emphasise that when the teacher thinks children are trying hard and keeping to the rules she will be quick to let them know and encourage them.

Any measures used are appropriate to the children, the situation and the misbehaviour

As with rewards, a teacher's selection of stronger measures, would be guided by her knowledge of the children, her relationship with them and the feasibility of different sanctions within her particular setting. The sanction used must match the misbehaviour which warranted it, or the teacher risks appearing unfair and causing resentment.

Stronger measures are used seldom and in the context of frequent attention and reward for 'good' behaviours

Remember to keep a praise-to-corrections ratio of 3:1 and preferably higher. Only when other corrections, including the warning procedure, have been tried unsuccessfully *or* when the misbehaviour is potentially harmful are sanctions brought into effect.

Stronger measures are used fairly and consistently

The teacher should be certain about *what* the misbehaviour is, its *effects* and *who* is misbehaving before implementing a sanction. Does the behaviour stop teaching or learning? If so, has a warning been given already? Are all members of group three involved or just Sonia and David? Is the behaviour really likely to cause harm? These questions involve a teacher being very alert to children's behaviour — and making some rapid but sound decisions. Warnings and sanctions should be used consistently over time and with different pupils.

Stronger measures are implemented without delay

Otherwise they might become consequences, not for the misbehaviour which warranted them, but for an entirely different behaviour, such as standing outside the staffroom waiting for the teacher!

Stronger measures are implemented clearly and firmly

They should be delivered without shouting, shaming or sarcasm. In specific circumstances it may be necessary to use gesture or physical prompts to guide the child (as may be the case with younger children). However, physical contact is generally inadvisable and any movements which are threatening (such as wild gestures, pushing, poking or hitting) must *always* be avoided. Otherwise the teacher risks losing authority, and increases the possibility of confrontation with the child. He would also be modelling behaviours which he would find unacceptable if his pupils followed his example.

The time and teacher attention involved are kept to a minimum

This enables a teacher to return his attention to the group and the lesson as quickly as possible and avoid the risk of reinforcing misbehaviour by giving it too much attention. Whilst adequate supervision is necessary, any counselling must be given at other times — when the child has behaved appropriately.

Once the child has complied with the warning or sanction the incident is treated as finished

The child may return to being part of the group and its activities. His teacher then makes two or three opportunities to praise him for appropriate behaviour.

Stronger measures are always used in conjunction with efforts to avoid the occurrence of serious misbehaviours. Prevention, for example by removing or protecting dangerous equipment, is an obvious step. A second is to set out to teach the acceptable behaviour which would be incompatible with a behaviour that is detrimental to learning, relationships and safety — for example, teaching children how to use potentially dangerous equipment safely, how to keep the rules and play appropriately with peers. This is consistent with the focus of a positive system of management upon *desired* behaviours.

SUMMARY

In Chapter 9 we have outlined different responses which a teacher

Table 9.5: Making constructive use of 'corrections'

Intervene as early as possible; all the corrections we described can be carried out there and then in the classroom

Use the lowest level of intervention necessary, according to the misbehaviour and its effects on learning, relationships and safety

Keep the time and attention given to misbehaviours to a minimum

Handle misbehaviours in a firm and matter-of-fact way; avoid showing unwanted behaviour yourself

Once dealt with, misbehaviours should be treated as finished; any counselling should take place at other times

Use all corrections consistently and fairly

Take active steps to teach and maintain appropriate behaviours; use far more rewards than corrections (a praise-to-corrections ratio of at least 3:1)

Use misbehaviours as pointers to improvements you can make in your classroom management

can make to unwanted behaviour (see Table 9.2) and offered some guidelines for their selection and use (summarised in Table 9.5).

When responding to undesired or inappropriate behaviours within a positive system of management, the outcomes the teacher seeks are always that misbehaviours are decreased and are replaced by appropriate behaviours; that lessons run smoothly and are productive and that a positive classroom atmosphere prevails. Within this framework unwanted behaviours can provide useful information, highlighting those aspects of classroom management which might be altered and improved.

10

Are Things Really As They Seem?

INTRODUCTION

Having identified an unwanted behaviour and taken steps to alter its circumstances or consequences in order to improve the way children behave, how do you know that your alterations are working? In this chapter we explain how you can gather information about changes in children's behaviour so as to evaluate what you are doing in class. Then we go on to consider the difficult question: when is 'unwanted' behaviour so serious as to be called a 'problem'? We outline ways in which a teacher can take a closer look at disturbing or intractable unwanted behaviours so as to assess whether they are as serious as they seem.

EVALUATING THE EFFECTS OF MANAGEMENT CHANGES

One way to tell that management changes are working is that the unwanted behaviour is no longer noticeable or irritating. A teacher might forget about it in its apparent absence. Another is that its alternative appropriate behaviour now seems more in evidence. All well and good, but these indications of improvement are based on subjective impressions. They may not reveal what is really going on. Moreover, since improvement in the children's behaviour may be slow and gradual, it would be easy to overlook small improvements. The teacher may then become disheartened, and suspect that alterations to the system have not 'worked'. The only accurate way to evaluate the success of changes made to the system is to *measure* their effects on children's behaviour over a period of time. Only in this way can you provide yourself, the children and others with the facts of the case.

That the behavioural approach lends itself to such objective measurement is one of its great strengths. Fairly complex observation schedules have been developed (see, for example, Wheldall, 1981) for sampling the behaviours of a group or individual within a class. Some of these also include observations of the teacher's behaviour (Wheldall and Merrett, 1984a). Another approach is to use video recordings (see, for example, Frankland, Pitchford and Pitchford, 1985). However in the absence of help from others — a student, perhaps, or a friendly and supportive colleague who may give up her only free period — such techniques would be impracticable.

There are a number of simple measures which are very feasible for one teacher to work alone and which will illustrate patterns of improvement over time. Many of these involve the use of evidence already to hand. Mark books, wall charts or individual records will show children's individual progress on educational tasks over time. These can give a cumulative record of the number of skills mastered, number of tasks completed on time, accuracy of work presented and so on. Given that your records are well-dated, you can then compare the children's performance before and since you implemented management changes. Similarly, if any kind of token system is used when working to improve classroom behaviours, the number of points scored can be tallied on a daily basis. For example, Mr Wright's records of his group game approach (see Chapter 9) might look something like Figure 10.1. House points, stars, beads, any kind of token used to reward either group or individual behaviour can be used to record progress over time in this way. Such records not only provide useful feedback for the teacher but can, and should, also be used to keep the children informed about their progress.

When working on only one or two behaviours it can be possible, without being distracting, for the teacher to count them as they occur. For example, if looking for in-seat behaviour it would be possible from time to time to check and count the number of children in their places at any one time. The totals can be jotted on paper, the mark book, or even the back of one's hand, to be recorded (as percentages of children present) later in the day. Similarly one could count the number of children who have, as required, started work within two minutes of the work being set, and record these day by day. Using a tally counter it is also possible to record the total instances of a particular behaviour over a period of time. In their training package for teachers Wheldall, Merrett and Russell (1983) advocate the use of a tally counter to measure one's *own* behaviour in class, as a way of ensuring that one is keeping the rate of positive

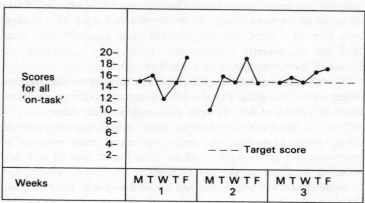

Figure 10.1: Daily scores on 20 observations in the 'on-task' behaviour game

and encouraging statements up and keeping the number of critical or corrective statements down.

Of course a teacher cannot be sure that the measures taken have been responsible for an improvement unless the records begin prior to the start of the intervention. For example, Mr Wright (see Chapter 9) could be deluding himself. The children may have been

Figure 10.2: Daily scores on 20 observations in the on-task behaviour game

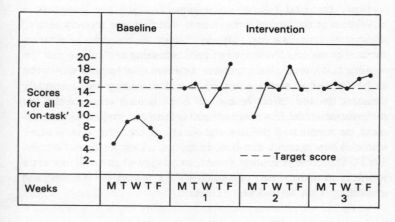

on-task as often *before* his group game as they were in the first few weeks. To overcome this problem, therefore, it is usual to take a *baseline* measure prior to instigating any changes which are designed to improve things. If Mr Wright had done so, he might have been even more satisfied with his game approach. As Figure 10.2 shows, baseline observations would have highlighted the effects of the group game on behaviour.

There are further benefits which can accrue from making baseline observations. It may be that the behaviour is not occurring with the frequency that was first thought. For example, one infant teacher, irritated by the fact that her pupils were 'always interrupting each other' during news sessions, decided to count actual instances of interruptions over several sessions. She found that in fact they occurred far less than she had expected.

Another teacher was concerned about a boy who swore a great deal in class. She was asked to record all instances of swearing over a period of a week. The next week she was surprised and pleased to find from her records that, after the first couple of days, the boy's swearing had dramatically decreased. In turning away to mark her tally sheet each time he swore, she had in fact withdrawn her attention at the right moment. His swearing had gone unreinforced and was well on the way to extinction, so that further types of intervention were already redundant.

In other situations, the teacher's noting of particular behaviours can be a sufficient clue to a fairly cooperative group and lead them to improve without intervention. Thus, whilst not always the case, this sort of approach can lead to interesting and useful benefits!

Now, the acid test of consequences which are designed to strengthen or to weaken behaviour is that they are actually seen to do so over time. We can only say, 'Stars are powerful reinforcers for this group' or, 'Now I've stopped attending to "calling out", it is going reinforced', if the children's pattern of behaviour shows this to be so. Only careful observation and recording can accurately demonstrate the effectiveness of a particular consequence for different children. If we subject children to our system of management, no matter how positive and wisely we feel it is used, we owe it to children to check that it is, in fact, working for them (Winter, 1982). Therefore recording should not be viewed as merely an extra job. It is an integral part of a teacher's framework for planning and evaluating what he is doing in class.

ASSESSING THE SERIOUSNESS OF A 'PROBLEM'

The process of measuring and recording behaviour is at no time more important then when planning and implementing systems for changing an individual's problem behaviours (Winter, 1982). The use of a behavioural approach with children who present problems of conduct or adjustment is very well documented, and has, perhaps, been the most common application of this model of behaviour. The techniques for behaviour change used with individuals who present difficult or problematic behaviours are also well documented, and it is beyond our remit to deal with them here. The principles are essentially as those outlined in the present book but applied more systematically, with greater consistency and precision, and employing techniques tailored specifically to the needs of individuals and groups within their particular setting (see, for example, Becker, Engelmann and Thomas, 1975; Leach and Raybould, 1977; Sulzer-Azaroff and Mayer, 1977; Vargas, 1977; Wheldall and Merrett, 1984b; Cheeseman and Watts, 1985).

We shall confine ourselves to the initial problem for the teacher dealing with a disturbing or intractable unwanted behaviour. That is, how to discern between a behaviour that is merely 'unwanted' and one that can be more properly described as a 'problem'. Children behave differently from each other and some present a teacher with more unwanted behaviours than others. However, there are occasions when a child's behaviour causes a teacher particular concern. It may be that a generally well-behaved child presents uncharacteristic and negative behaviours. Or a child may already have a reputation for bad behaviour which he brings with him on transfer to the class. It may be that, when most of the children are responding well to your system of management, there are one or two individuals of whom you feel, 'I cannot reach them'. No-one wishes to overreact, and yet one is reluctant to do nothing when there may be some way in which teacher, school, or others can help. Here we offer some guidelines as to how a teacher can begin to assess the seriousness of a child's unwanted behaviour (adapted from Leach and Raybould, 1977). The steps involved are shown in Table 10.1.

Step 1: ask yourself some pertinent questions

First and foremost you must think about your own reactions to a child's behaviour. Now, more than at any other time, it is important

Table 10.1: Assessing the seriousness of a child's unwanted behaviour

Step 1	Ask yourself some pertinent questions
Step 2	Define the behaviour which worries you
Step 3	Observe the behaviour — its frequency, duration and reasonableness
Step 4	Compare the child's behaviour with that of his peers
Step 5	Assess the effects of the behaviour on the child's activities and those of others
Step 6	Estimate other pupils' acceptance — of the behaviour and the child
Step 7	Try to identify relevant factors in the environment
Step 8	Find out how widespread the difficulties are — the generality and number of unwanted behaviours

to try and distinguish between the behaviour and its effects as external events, and the personal feelings the behaviour arouses in you. Ask yourself what it is that you find so annoying or worrying about this child's behaviour. Could it be that your judgement is affected by the child's appearance, your knowledge of his background or assumptions about his 'intelligence'? You will need to ask yourself whether it is just you — are you personally 'allergic' to this sort of behaviour? Teachers are not superhuman. They cannot like and get along well with every single child they meet; nor can they please all of their pupils all of the time. Do you need to recognise that there could be a 'personality clash' here?

By asking yourself such questions you can begin to tease out the influence which *your own* feelings and attitudes have in colouring your interpretation of, and reactions to, a child's behaviour.

Step 2: define the behaviour which worries you

Avoid the temptation to label the behaviour with terms like 'aggressive' and 'disruptive'. Pin yourself down to a specific description of what the child does which causes concern, then you will be in a position to check out your subjective impressions by making observations. You will know what you are looking for.

Step 3: observe the behaviour

Observing the behaviour as it occurs over just one or two days can be misleading. It is safer to make observations, and to keep note of them, over a period of at least a week or two.

How often?

Behaviours may cause concern because they seem to occur too often. Conversely it may be the absence of a behaviour which worries you as in, for example, a child who does not seem to interact with his peers. In both cases check the *actual* frequency, by counting the number of times the behaviour occurs or fails to occur when expected.

How long each time?

Other behaviours cause concern because, although they do not occur often, they continue for too long. For example, temper tantrums from a nursery school child may be over quickly, but if the child screams for lengthy periods this can turn an 'unwanted' behaviour into a 'problem' behaviour. The most accurate observation is to time the duration of the behaviour when it occurs.

How reasonable?

Is the behaviour a reasonable response to the situation in which it occurs? In some instances a child may be expected to react in this way, given the circumstances; in others the reaction may be out of all proportion to the events preceding it.

Step 4: compare the child's behaviour with that of his peers

How does the frequency or duration of the behaviour compare with the way children of similar age behave? It may be that this behaviour is quite common in the child's class or year. Alternatively it may be very unusual in comparison with the peer group. Does the child really stand out from other children in his class or year group?

Step 5: assess the effects of the behaviour

Note the extent to which the unwanted behaviour interferes with the child's activities and those of others.

Interference with the child's activities

Depending on the *intensity* of the behaviour it may only marginally affect the child's other activities or it may disrupt them altogether. For example, while a child is in a tantrum or is curled up, crying, beneath her desk other activities are virtually precluded!

167

Effects on other's activities

Behaviours may differ in their disruptive effects on the group's classroom activities or upon other children's play at breaktimes. Are such activities interrupted by the occurrence of the child's unwanted behaviour briefly, for longer periods, or might whole lessons be in jeopardy? How many other pupils are affected by the child's behaviour?

Step 6: estimate other pupils' acceptance

It is important to assess the effects which the behaviour has on the child's relationships with other pupils. Do they continue to relate positively to him? Do they avoid him or complain when he behaves in this way? Is he often excluded from their play? Do they blame him for things he actually did not do?

Step 7: try to identify relevant factors in the environment

Since factors within the context for the behaviour may well contribute towards its occurrence, it is important to take note of where and when the behaviour occurs. For example it may be that the child's present tasks in a certain subject area are too difficult for her. Moreover, the unwanted behaviour may be maintained by its immediate consequences, perhaps even by your own attention!

It is therefore important to take note of where and when the behaviour occurs and the events which precede and follow it. If you are then able to identify factors in the environment which possibly contribute towards the behaviour, you will be in a position to consider what changes you could make in your management to improve matters. On the other hand, the more difficulty there is in identifying factors within the setting events and consequences, the more seriously the unwanted behaviour must be viewed.

Step 8: find out how widespread the difficulties are

The seriousness you attach to the behaviour which worries you will often depend on how general the behaviour is and how many other unwanted behaviours the child shows in school.

Generality

The behaviour may be specific to a particular situation or may occur across a number of different situations and with different people.

The number of unwanted behaviours

Does the child show only one behaviour which gives concern in school or does he display many different kinds of difficult behaviour?

You will need to consult with colleagues to assess these aspects of a child's behaviour. If you seek colleagues' information and views, make sure you avoid leading questions which merely seek the other's confirmation of your perceptions. In discussion, be as specific about the behaviour as you can to ensure that you are both talking about the same thing!

Having made your observations and sought information from others, you can assess the relative seriousness of the problem on each of the dimensions outlined above. You might draw up a summary of your findings (see for example the format illustrated in Table 10.2) then add your comments as to the seriousness you attach to them.

Table 10.2: Assessing the seriousness of an unwanted behaviour: summarising your findings

Dimension	Findings	Comments
Frequency		
Duration		
Reasonableness		
Comparison with peers		
Interference with child's activities		
Interference with others' activities		
Other pupils' acceptance		
Possible environmental factors		
Generality		
Number of 'unwanted' behaviours		

To offer specific suggestions as to the cut-off point at which a behaviour turns from 'unwanted' to 'problem' on these various dimensions could be misleading. Thus the seriousness attached to the frequency or duration of the behaviour will depend on the behaviour and its circumstances, and similar qualifications could be added for each of the dimensions we have considered.

Moreover, the judgement of a behaviour as 'serious' on certain dimensions, such as its interference with class activities, may be offset by the ease with which the teacher can identify possible contributing factors in the environment and makes changes to these. In general, we could expect that the more dimensions on which an unwanted behaviour is judged to be 'serious' the more likely that it is a 'problem' particularly if it results in non-acceptance by peers or is one of a number of difficult behaviours shown in school. Even here though, there may be exceptions. For example, an unwanted behaviour may not be serious in its effects on the child's relationships nor occur in many situations. However, it might be repeated so often in *some* situations that it is a 'problem' behaviour on the grounds of its frequency alone.

It is therefore for you to assess the seriousness of unwanted behaviours shown by your pupils within your school and classroom environment. If you follow the suggestions we have outlined, they may help you to disentangle the feelings which a child's behaviour promotes in you and achieve a clearer assessment of what is going on. They may also help in structuring discussions with colleagues and parents about appropriate and helpful courses of action that might be taken.

SUMMARY

In Chapter 10 we considered ways in which a teacher can take a closer look at behaviour and events in class to find out if things are really as they seem. We discussed some ways to evaluate the changes made to classroom management when dealing with undesired behaviour and some of the reasons why evaluation is important. We also described steps a teacher can take to assess the relative seriousness of a child's unwanted behaviour.

A behavioural approach enables us to make a more objective and accurate assessment of classroom events. It assists us to check that management changes *are* working for the benefit of pupils and helps put difficult and worrying problems in perspective.

11

Handing Over the Reins

INTRODUCTION

We have now described the components of a *positive system of management*. We began by considering how the physical, social and educational setting events can be arranged to promote children's appropriate behaviour in the classroom. This was followed by discussions on managing the consequences provided for children's behaviour. We described different types of rewards together with guidelines for their use in teaching and strengthening appropriate behaviours. Particular attention was drawn to the importance of 'natural' consequences in maintaining desirable behaviours once they have become established. Then, since unwanted behaviours will invariably appear we also outlined ways in which a teacher can respond to them and decrease their frequency.

Whilst we have considered these different aspects of management separately, they are integral parts of the same systematic approach. Managed effectively they work together to establish those behaviours we judge to be appropriate in the context of a particular classroom environment. However, a system of management must have long-term goals for children, as well as the immediate, shorter-term goals of establishing behaviours which are desirable in the here and now of their present class. The system would fall short of requirements if its effectiveness in maintaining children's appropriate behaviour was entirely dependent on a particular type of classroom setting or a certain teacher. Under those circumstances children's 'good' behaviour might well break down with a new teacher, different classroom or novel activities.

Children's behaviour must ultimately be weaned away from a dependence upon their teacher and her careful management of

171

setting events and consequences. In time pupils must continue to behave in acceptable ways with other teachers and beyond their immediate classroom environment. Thus, the system of management must teach them to *generalise* their appropriate behaviour. Furthermore, the ultimate objective is for each child's 'good' behaviour to be maintained because it is governed by his or her own *personal control*. The system must therefore help children learn to monitor and regulate their own behaviour.

We therefore conclude this book by considering how a teacher, using a positive system of management, might be seen as working towards these longer-term goals. We outline which features of the system have particular importance at different stages of learning, from learning new behaviours through to developing personal control. Finally, we highlight the interactive nature of behaviour. Your behaviour as a teacher is influenced by environmental factors too and whilst the children are learning from you, you are also learning from them!

WORKING TOWARDS LONGER-TERM GOALS

Here we develop some of the points made in Chapters 7 and 8 and discuss how different aspects of a positive system of management work together to help children generalise appropriate behaviour and develop personal control.

Towards generalisation

We would highlight two processes which contribute towards generalisation: establishing 'natural' outcomes as rewarding consequences for children's 'good' behaviour and increasing the control of setting events over behaviour.

Establishing natural reinforcers

Initially a teacher might use a range of rewards for children's behaviour which she anticipates to be already motivating for the children. However, many of these rewards, for example giving stars for educational progress, are not the natural outcomes of the behaviour which is being taught. They are more 'artificial' or specially arranged. We have stressed the need always to associate any rewards which a teacher specially arranges with their more naturally occurring counterparts. The intention is that the natural rewards will themselves come to have value for children, through their association with events or things which are already rewarding. When a teacher gives a child feedback, she is pointing out not only what the child did that was appropriate but what was achieved, for example in terms of success or improvement in his work. She is helping him to see the natural outcome of his behaviour.

In this way a teacher helps children to notice and value those consequences which occur naturally through their work and other people's behaviour towards them. The intention is that once appropriate social behaviours and work habits are established, the teacher can gradually withdraw other rewards. Children's appropriate behaviours should then continue to be encouraged and maintained by their natural consequences, rather than being dependent on the teacher's behaviour or the special rewards she can arrange.

Increasing the influence of setting events

The pleasant consequences of desired behaviour have two roles. They confirm that the behaviour they follow was indeed appropriate and they strengthen the connection between setting events and the behaviour. They increase the likelihood that the setting events will cue the appropriate behaviour in the future. Conversely when behaviour is inappropriate, non-desired consequences weaken the connection between setting events and the unwanted behaviour. The consequences decrease the likelihood that these setting events will cue the unwanted behaviour in future.

Provided that a teacher manages the consequences of children's behaviour consistently over time she enhances the influence of setting events over their behaviour. For instance, by consistently praising children for following classroom rules and ignoring them when they do not, she increases the influence that classroom rules will have as cues for children's future behaviour.

When children's wanted and unwanted behaviour is managed consistently in differing situations, the teacher helps children to *discriminate* between the cues provided by different setting events. For example, they may talk during some activities but not others; they may run during PE but not during music, although both lessons may well be held in the hall. Consistency between consequences from different sources is also vital if children are to receive an unambiguous message. Hence the value of approaches like the 'group game' which work to ensure consistency between the responses of both teacher and classmates to pupils' appropriate and inappropriate behaviour.

Consequences then must be managed consistently but what about the management of setting events? When teaching new behaviour or responses to new situations we have noted that consistency between setting events is also important. Thus the classroom and events within it must all point in the same way: to the desired behaviour. However, once appropriate behaviour becomes well established, the need for this degree of consistency is lessened. Indeed it is advantageous to introduce variation for we do not want children to present appropriate behaviour only when everything around them directs them to do so. We would like pupils to generalise their behaviour to other similar settings, such as other classrooms, the library and, perhaps later, to working at home. Similarly, we do not wish children to rely solely on the teacher for directions on how to complete their work. They must learn how to follow written instructions and cues present *within* the task so that they can work independently. Setting events must be arranged consistently over time when teaching new behaviour. However, they can be varied once the behaviour is well established so that children learn to discriminate between different features of the setting events and to follow those which are the *critical* features in governing their behaviour. In this way behaviour generalises to other work places, to different teachers and to new learning activities.

Generalisation enables children to respond to new situations and learning experiences which they have not previously encountered. Varying the setting events for well-established appropriate behaviour is an integral part of this process. However, it is vital that children's behaviour *continues* to be maintained by its consequences. First, desirable and naturally occurring consequences must be available from a number of different sources within the school. Secondly, children must be encouraged to appreciate intrinsic rewards that can follow directly from their appropriate behaviour.

Towards personal control

A teacher begins work towards children's regulation of their own behaviour in three ways:

(1) by establishing natural outcomes as reinforcers for behaviour;
(2) by providing feedback which links behaviour to its setting events and consequences;
(3) by offering children choices.

As we have already discussed the process by which natural consequences become reinforcing, we shall concentrate here on the effects of feedback and pupil choice.

Feedback

When the teacher draws children's attention to a particular behaviour, its outcomes and the setting events in which it occurs, he enables them to make these links between their behaviour and its surrounding events for themselves. This feedback helps children to learn more quickly than they would do on their own. They can begin to notice their own behaviour and to appreciate that their actions have effects. In this way the teacher prepares the ground for children to recognise responsibility for their own behaviour.

Pupil choice

Once pupils are able to monitor the effects of their behaviour the teacher can help them to anticipate the possible outcomes of their actions and to make choices about how to respond in particular circumstances. Children often have a number of options about how to behave at a given time. A teacher can assist them towards making these choices for themselves by pointing out or eliciting from the children what the alternative consequences of each behaviour would be. When the outcomes of alternative actions are clear, the teacher can give the children opportunities to decide what to do. The consequences are then determined *by the children* and they take responsibility for their choice. For example, pupils may make certain decisions about the order in which they will undertake particular activities during an 'integrated' session. They will need to anticipate the choices made by others to avoid a crush at certain activities, and they take responsibility for satisfactorily completing all the tasks listed by the end of the session. In other situations children will be given responsibility for organising an entire piece of work, for instance when undertaking an individual topic or a small group project.

At times children may be permitted to work in places that are beyond their teacher's direct supervision, for example in a different area of the open-plan base or in other parts of the school. Within reason, pupils might even be allowed to choose where the best place would be to work on a particular task. These situations may require consultation with colleagues. They always require the teacher's confidence that the children can and will behave well during their absence. They involve the final test of children's personal control of their behaviour — temptation!

Feedback assists children towards monitoring their own behaviour and its outcomes in different circumstances. It enables children to see that their behaviour can and does influence events and this carries implications about their own responsibility for their actions. The teacher encourages children to begin making choices and decisions for themselves by helping them to anticipate the possible outcomes of their actions and by providing pupils with choices about their own activities. Finally, by teaching children the value of natural consequences and particularly of those which are intrinsic to their behaviour she enables pupils to gain their own rewards for behaving in appropriate ways. The ultimate intention is that children will remain interested in their schoolwork for its own sake and derive satisfaction from relating positively towards other people.

We have stressed that generalisation and personal control of behaviour are long-term goals which, in some situations, may seem quite remote from the stage at which a teacher and her pupils are presently working. Let us now attempt to place them in context by considering the different levels at which a positive system of management might be applied.

LINKING THE SYSTEM TO DIFFERENT STAGES OF LEARNING

Depending on the ages of your pupils, their previous experience of your type of classroom organisation and your initial estimations of what can be expected of them in class, you can apply a positive system of management at different levels.

At the beginning of a year with a new group, and particularly when starting out with very young children, the immediate priority is to teach and to strengthen those behaviours which are appropriate to your particular situation. As appropriate behaviours become established in response to your classroom routines and activities the focus will be upon maintaining 'good' behaviour with suitable natural consequences.

With older pupils, who are 'old hands' at basic routines and procedures, or during the latter stages of a school year, appropriate behaviour is more likely to be well-maintained by natural consequences. Children's appropriate behaviour will now be increasingly influenced by cues from the classroom and the setting events within it, and generalisation can be encouraged. Furthermore, once behaviours are well-established in response to familiar setting events and are maintained by natural consequences, the shift away from dependence on your management and towards children's personal control can begin. Responsibility for behaviour management can increasingly be shared with the children themselves, both as individuals and as a group.

The different features of a positive system of management which are particularly relevant at these stages are summarised in Table 11.1.

Of course in the real world, with a class group of 25–30 children, transfer from one stage in learning to another does not follow such a unified and clearcut sequence. Different children may be at different stages of learning particular types of behaviour. Some children in the group may work for natural consequences on entry to your class whilst others may need additional reinforcers and feedback to get them onto natural social or curriculum-based reinforcers. Furthermore, whilst some classroom behaviours will be well-established others that are specific to your situation will need to be taught from the outset. If you change your organisation to, say, an integrated-day system, you will need to teach the new rules and routines associated with this pattern of organisation. Thus the system may operate at different levels according to the stage of the year, the different behaviours you expect and the skill levels that children have reached.

There is no easy solution that we can offer to assist your decisions as to which level to pitch your system with a particular class. This is very much for you to decide on the basis of your experience and, most important of all, your assessment of the children's behaviour at different stages of the year. Use their previous records and your knowledge of their previous teacher's organisation to help in your initial estimation of children's skills and your expectations at the outset. Then pitch in!

Table 11.1: Linking the system to different stages of learning

Stage	Characteristics	Salient features of the system
I New and weak behaviours	Children are learning entirely new behaviours appropriate to your classroom and organisation Other desired behaviours are weak in response to new routines, instructions and so on Unwanted behaviours may occur	Planned and consistent setting events making full use of rules, routines, physical cues and prompts Choice of appropriate rewards and finding out existing ones which are effective Giving rewards *and* feedback for appropriate behaviours often and consistently (i.e. with setting events; over time and across pupils) Pointing out natural outcomes of behaviour
II Maintaining behaviour	Appropriate behaviours are frequent and are established in response to familiar setting events and in the presence of existing reinforcers Some unwanted behaviours prove tenacious, particularly among some individuals	Rewards arranged by the teacher are gradually faded to a more occasional and intermittent pattern as the shift to natural rewards (educational and social outcomes) is encouraged Whilst reward type changes and their frequency is reduced, consistent management of consequences must be sustained Tenacious unwanted behaviours will highlight adjustments to setting events and/or consequences as necessary for the group or individuals
III Generalisation	Appropriate behaviours are well-established and children may begin behaviours prior to specific cues given by the teacher Appropriate behaviours are sustained in presence of conflicting cues (for example, individual task and table seating)	Establish links between the essential cues in the setting events and the desired behaviour Changes in other features of the setting events are made so that essential cues govern behaviour (for example, seating arrangements are more flexible; teacher instructions are less precise; children work independently on practice tasks)
IV Developing personal control	Children anticipate events They exert influence to prevent or interrupt unwanted behaviours by others They behave appropriately in absence of supervision or teacher direction They show appropriate behaviours in a number of different settings and situations They show initiative and independence on tasks They seek responsibility in personal and class organisation	Point out links between behaviour and consequences Point out alternative consequences and help children decide what to do Give pupils increased responsibility for organisation of work and for task completion Involve children in discussions on class organisation, rules, etc. Give pupils increasing trust — to work with reduced supervision and in different locations

SUMMARY: LEARNING THROUGH PRACTICE

In this book we have applied the behavioural model to the management of children's behaviour in class.

This approach provides a framework for consistent management which stresses the importance of helping children to show appropriate behaviours from the outset, rather than waiting for them to happen. However, a positive system of management is not concerned only with the short-term objectives of teaching children behaviours that are desirable and constructive in their immediate situation.

We have considered how the various integral parts of the system work together to help children sustain and generalise their behaviour to new situations and to take personal control of their behaviour.

Throughout we have concentrated on the *teacher's* behaviour — both prior to and during contact time. We have illustrated the ways in which the teacher's behaviour influences that of the children through her management of the physical, social and educational components of the classroom environment. In many cases this involves direct interactions between the behaviour of teacher and pupils. For instance, the teacher gives instructions, the children behave in appropriate ways and the teacher praises them for doing so. In many other cases the influence of teacher behaviour is less direct, operating for example through her arrangement of the room, her selection and patterning of educational tasks and her organisation of the group's activities.

Just as the children's behaviour is influenced by environmental factors, so too is that of their teacher. The classroom setting and events within it will operate to cue behaviours from you and to provide consequences for your behaviour, much as they do for the children. Of course the cues you follow, the behaviour with which you respond and the consequences for your behaviour will differ from those of the children! Nevertheless you will inevitably be learning new behaviours. Certain behaviours will be maintained and others weakened and it is to be hoped that you will generalise those behaviours which work well for you in one situation to others in a different classroom and with different children.

For the most part it is the behaviour and progress of your pupils which provide you with consequences for your own 'classroom behaviour'. You have aims and goals for their behaviour and progress. You are rewarded with pleasant consequences when they behave as desired, when they achieve the next step in the curriculum and when their behaviour suggests enjoyment of the activities you have planned. Conversely, your behaviour as a teacher is likely to be subject to checks and balances provided by children's unwanted behaviour, slow progress or lack of interest.

Our book is offered as a contribution to the setting events for *your own* behaviour in managing children's behaviour in class. We would urge you to practise the principles and techniques we have described — in as many and varied situations as you can and as consistently as you can. We hope they help you to enhance your existing good practice, or to learn new classroom management skills, more quickly than you would by learning alone through your personal experiences in the classroom.

We hope too, that by applying the principles of the positive system of management to your planning and implementation of classroom practice you will find satisfaction and pleasure in the ways your pupils respond to you, to each other and to their work.

References

Ainscow, M. and Tweddle, D.A. (1979) *Preventing Classroom Failure*, Wiley, Chichester.

Albert, S. and Dabbs, J.M. (1970) 'Physical distance and persuasion', *Journal of Personality and Social Psychology*, 15, 265–70, cited by Bell, Fisher and Loomis (1978).

Arlin, M. (1979) 'Teacher transitions can disrupt time flow in classrooms', *American Educational Research Journal*, 16 (1), 42–56, cited in Gnagey (1981).

Barker-Lunn, J.C. (1970) *Streaming in the Primary School*, National Foundation for Educational Research, Slough.

Becker, W.C., Engelmann, S. and Thomas, D.R. (1975) *Teaching 1: Classroom Management*, Science Research Associates, Chicago.

Bell, P.A., Fisher, J.D. and Loomis, R.J. (1978) *Environmental Psychology*, W.B. Saunders Co., Philadelphia.

Brophy, J.E. and Evertson, G.M. (1976) *Learning From Teaching: A Developmental Perspective*, Allyn and Bacon, Boston.

Burns, R. (1982) *Self-Concept Development and Education*, Holt, Rinehart and Winston, London.

Cheeseman, P.L. and Watts, P.E. (1985) *Positive Behaviour Management: A Manual for Teachers*, Croom Helm, London.

Clarizio, H.F.C. (1980) *Towards Positive Classroom Discipline*, 3rd edn, John Wiley, New York.

Department of Education and Science (1972) *Standards for School Premises Regulations 1972*, HMSO, London.

Department of Education and Science (1981a) *Lighting and Acoustic Criteria for the Visually Handicapped and Hearing Impaired in Schools*, Design Note 25, DES, London.

Department of Education and Science (1981b) *Guidelines for Environmental Design and Fuel Conservation in Educational Buildings*, Design Note 17, DES, London.

Department of Education and Science (1984) *Designing for Children with Special Educational Needs (Ordinary Schools)*, Building Bulletin 61, HMSO, London.

Donaldson, M. (1978) *Children's Minds*, Fontana, Glasgow.

Edwards, D.J.A. (1972) 'Approaching the unfamiliar: a study of human interaction distances', *Journal of Behavioural Sciences*, 1, 249–50, cited by Bell, Fisher and Loomis (1978).

Elashoff, J. and Snow, R.E. (1971) *Pygmalion Reconsidered*, Jones, Ohio.

Frankland, S., Pitchford, Y. and Pitchford, M. (1985) 'The use of video-recording to provide repeated monitoring of the successful use of 'rules, praise and ignoring' with a class of 14–15 year olds in a comprehensive school', *Behavioural Approaches with Children*, 9 (3) 67–78.

Gannaway, H. (1976) 'Making sense of school' in M. Stubbs and S. Delamont (eds.) *Explorations in Classroom Observation*, John Wiley and Sons Ltd, London, pp. 45–82.

181

Glynn, T. (1982) 'Antecedent control of behaviour in educational contexts', *Educational Psychology*, **2** (3–4), 215–29.

Gnagey, W.J. (1981) *Motivating Classroom Discipline*, Macmillan, New York.

Gronlund, N.E. (1970) *Stating Behavioural Objectives for Classroom Instruction*, Macmillan, New York.

Guardo, C.J. (1969) 'Personal space in children', *Child Development*, **40**, 143–51, cited by Porteous (1977).

Hall, E.T. (1966) *The Hidden Dimension*, Doubleday, New York.

Hargreaves, D.H. (1972) *Interpersonal Relations and Education*, Routledge, London.

Haring, N.G. and Eaton, M.D. (1978) 'Systematic Instructional Procedures: An Instructional Hierarchy', in N.G. Haring *et al.*, *The Fourth R — Research In The Classroom*, Charles E. Merrill, Columbus, Ohio, pp. 23–40.

Heshka, S. and Nelson, Y. (1972) 'Interpersonal speaking distance as a function of age, sex and relationship', *Sociometry*, **35**, 491–8, cited by Bell, Fisher and Loomis (1978).

Institute of Advanced Architectural Studies (1976) *A Right to be Children: Designing for the Education of the Under-Fives*, RIBA, London.

Johnson, D.W. and Johnson, R.T. (1975) *Learning Together and Alone*, Prentice-Hall, Englewood Cliffs, New Jersey.

Kounin, J.S. (1970) 'Discipline and group management in classrooms', Holt, Rinehart and Winston, New York, cited in Gnagey (1981).

Krantz, P.J. and Risley, T.R. (1977) 'Behavioural ecology in the classroom', in O'Leary, K.D. (ed.) *Classroom Management: The Successful Use of Behaviour Modification*, 2nd edn, Pergamon Press, New York.

Leach, D.J. and Raybould, E.C. (1977) *Learning and Behaviour Difficulties in School*, Open Books Publishing Ltd., London.

McIntire, R.W. (1974) 'Guidelines for using behaviour modification in education', in R. Ulrich, T. Stachnik and J. Mabry (eds), *Control of Human Behaviour. Behaviour Modification in Education*, **3**, Scott, Foresman and Co., Glenview, Illinois, pp. 408–13.

McNaughton, S. (1981) 'Low progress readers and teacher instructional behaviour during oral reading: the risk of maintaining instructional dependence' *The Exceptional Child*, **28** (3), 167–76.

McNaughton, S. and Glynn, T. (1981) 'Delayed versus immediate attention to oral reading errors: effects on accuracy and self correction', *Educational Psychology*, **1** (1) 57–63.

Mager, R.F. (1962) *Preparing Instructional Objectives*, Fearon Publishers, Belmont, California.

Manning, P. (ed.) (1967) *The Primary School: An Environment for Education*, Pilkington Research Unit, Department of Building Science, University of Liverpool.

Marland, M. (1975) *The Craft of the Classroom*, Heinemann Educational Books Ltd., London.

Medland, M. and Vitale, M. (1984) *Management of Classrooms*, CBS College of Publishing. Holt, Rinehart and Winston, New York.

Merrett, F.E. and Wheldall, K. (1978) 'Playing the game: a behavioural approach to classroom management in the junior school', *Educational Review*, **30** (1), 41–9.

Moore, D. (1980) 'Location as a causal factor in the unequal distribution of teacher questions: an experimental analysis', *Behaviour Therapy in Australia, Proceedings of the Third Australian Conference on Behaviour Modification*, 316–24, Melbourne. May, cited by Glynn (1982).

Moore, D.W. (1982) 'Variation in teacher question rate as a function of position in the classroom', paper presented at the Fifth National Conference on Behaviour Modification, Surfers Paradise, Queensland, cited by Glynn (1982).

Peter, L.J. (1977) *Quotations for Our Time*, Methuen Paperbacks Ltd., London.

Pidgeon, D.A. (1970) *Expectations and Pupil Performance*, NFER, London.

Porteous, J. Douglas (1977) *Environment and Behaviour: Planning and Everyday Urban Life*, Addison-Wesley Publishing Co. USA

Robertson, J. (1981) *Effective Classroom Control*, Hodder and Stoughton, Sevenoaks, Kent.

Rosenthal, R. and Jacobson, L. (1968) *Pygmalion in the Classroom*, Holt, Rinehart and Winston, New York.

Ruff, A. R. (1981) *Commercial and Industrial Law*, 2nd edn, Macdonald and Evans Ltd., Plymouth.

Russo, N. (1967) 'Connotations of seating arrangements', *Cornell Journal of Social Relations*, **2**, 37–44, cited by Sommer (1969).

Scherer, S.E. (1974) 'Proxemic behaviour of primary school children as a function of their socio-economic class and subculture', *Journal of Personality and Social Psychology*, **29**, 800–5, cited by Bell, Fisher and Loomis (1978).

Solity, J.E. (in preparation) 'The use of rules in effective classroom management'.

Solity, J.E. and Bull, S.L. (1987) *Special Needs: Bridging the Curriculum Gap*, Open University Press, Milton Keynes.

Sommer, R. (1969) *Personal Space: the Behavioural Basis of Design*, Prentice-Hall, Englewood Cliffs, New Jersey.

Sommer, R. (1974) *Tight Spaces Hard Architecture and How to Humanize It*, Prentice-Hall, Englewood Cliffs, New Jersey.

Sommer, R. and Olsen, H. (1980) 'The soft classroom', *Environment and Behaviour*, **12** (1) 3–16.

Stubbs, M. (1976) 'Keeping in touch: some functions of teacher-talk', in M. Stubbs and S. Delamont (eds) *Explorations in Classroom Observation*, John Wiley and Sons, London, pp. 151–72.

Sulzer-Azaroff, B. and Mayer, G.R. (1977) *Applying Behaviour — Analysis Procedures with Children and Youth*, Holt, Rinehart and Winston, New York.

Sundstrom, E. (in collaboration with Sundstrom, M.G.) (1986) *Work Places: the Psychology of the Physical Environment in Offices and Factories*, Cambridge University Press, New York.

Tizard, B. and Hughes, M. (1984) *Young Children Learning*, Fontana, London.

Topping, K. and Wolfendale, S. (1985) *Parental Involvement in Children's*

Reading, Croom Helm, London.

Torode, B. (1976) 'Teachers' talk and classroom discipline', in M. Stubbs and S. Delamont (eds), *Explorations in Classroom Observation*, John Wiley and Sons Ltd., London, pp. 173–92.

Tough, J. (1976a) *Listening to Children Talking: A Guide to the Appraisal of Children's Use of Language*, Ward Lock Educational, London.

Tough, J. (1976b) *The Development of Meaning: A Study of Children's Use of Language*, Allen and Unwin, London.

Tough, J. (1977) *Talking and Learning: A Guide to Fostering Communication Skills in Nursery and Infant Schools*, Ward Lock Educational, London.

Vargas, J.S. (1977) *Behavioural Psychology for Teachers*, Harper and Row, New York.

Walker, R. and Adelman, C. (1976) 'Strawberries', in M. Stubbs and S. Delamont (eds), *Explorations in Classroom Observation*, John Wiley and Sons Ltd., London, pp.133–50.

Weinstein, C.S. and Woolfolk, A.E. (1981) 'The classroom setting as a source of expectations about teachers and pupils', *Journal of Environmental Psychology*, **1**, 117–29.

Wells, G. (1978) "Language use and educational success": an empirical response to Joan Tough's development of meaning', *Research in Education*, **18**, 9–34.

Wheldall, K. (1981) 'Concluding comments: A before C or the use of behavioural ecology in the classroom', in K. Wheldall (ed.), *The Behaviourist in the Classroom: Aspects of Applied Behavioural Analysis in British Educational Contexts*, Chapter 14, Educational Review Offset Publications No. 2. University of Birmingham.

Wheldall, K. and Merrett, F.E. (1984a) 'Training teachers to be more positive', in S.N. Bennett and C.W. Desforges (eds) *Recent Advances in Classroom Research*, Monograph of the British Journal of Educational Psychology, Scottish Academic Press in association with the British Psychological Society, Edinburgh.

Wheldall, K. and Merrett, D.E. (1984b) *Positive Teaching: the Behavioural Approach*, George Allen and Unwin, London.

Wheldall, K., Merrett, P. and Russell, A. (1983) *The Behavioural Approach to Teaching Package*, a research project funded by Schools Council, 1981–83, University of Birmingham.

White, P.G., Solity, J.E. and Reeve, C.J. (1984) 'Teaching parents to teach reading', *Special Education/Forward Trends*, **11**, 11–13.

Willis, F.N. (1966) 'Initial speaking distance as a function of the speakers' relationship', *Psychonomic Science*, **5**, 221–2, cited by Porteous (1977) and Bell, Fisher and Loomis (1978).

Winter, S. (1982) 'Why measure behaviour?', *Educational Psychology*, **2**, (3–4), 185–95.

Wragg, E.C. (ed.) (1984) *Classroom Teaching Skills*, Croom Helm, London.

Suggested Further Reading

Becker, W.C., Engelmann, S. and Thomas, D.R. (1975) *Teaching 1: Classroom Management*, Science Research Associates, Chicago.

Cheeseman, P.L. and Watts, P.E. (1985) *Positive Behaviour Management: A Manual for Teachers*, Croom Helm, London.

Glynn, T. (1982) 'Antecedent Control of Behaviour in Educational Contexts', *Educational Psychology*, 2 (3–4), 215–29.

Johnson, D.W. and Johnson, R.T. (1975) *Learning Together and Alone*, Prentice-Hall, Englewood Cliffs, New Jersey.

Leach, D.J. and Raybould, E.C. (1977) *Learning and Behaviour Difficulties in School*, Open Books Publishing Ltd., London.

Lovitt, T.C. (1977) *In Spite of My Resistance . . . I've Learned from Children*, Charles E. Merrill, Columbus, Ohio.

Medland, M. and Vitale, M. (1984) *Management of Classrooms*, CBS College Publishing. Holt, Rinehart and Winston, New York.

O'Leary, K.D. and O'Leary, S.G. (1977) *Classroom Management. The Successful Use of Behaviour Modification*. Pergamon Press, Oxford.

Robertson, J. (1981) *Effective Classroom Control*, Hodder and Stoughton, Sevenoaks, Kent.

Solity, J.E. and Bull, S.L. (1987) *Special Needs: Bridging the Curriculum Gap*, Open University Press, Milton Keynes.

Sommer, R. (1969) *Personal Space: the Behavioural Basis of Design*, Prentice-Hall, Englewood Cliffs, New Jersey.

Sulzer-Azaroff, B. and Mayer, G.R. (1977) *Applying Behaviour — Analysis Procedures with Children and Youth*, Holt, Rinehart and Winston, New York.

Vargas, J. (1977) *Behavioural Psychology for Teachers*, Harper and Row, New York.

Wheldall, K. (ed.) (1981) *The Behaviourist in the Classroom*, Educational Review Offset Publications No. 2, University of Birmingham.

Wheldall, K. and Merrett, F.E. (1984) *Positive Teaching: The Behavioural Approach*, George Allen and Unwin, London.

Wragg, E.C. (ed.) (1984) *Classroom Teaching Skills*, Croom Helm, London.

Index